ANDY WOULDN'T LET ME

ANDY WOULDN'T LET ME

◆

Football vs. Fate

Bryan Kennedy

with

Langdon Reid

BRYAN-KENNEDY ENTERTAINMENT, LLC

ANDY WOULDN'T LET ME

PUBLISHED BY: BRYAN KENNEDY & LANGDON REID

through

BRYAN-KENNEDY ENTERTAINMENT, LLC

P.O. Box 1324
Franklin, TN 37065
800.284.9939
Email@Bryan-Kennedy.com

P.O. Box 2834
Staunton, VA 24402
www.WinkAtLife.com

ISBN: 978-0-615-34699-1

Printed in the United States

Cover design by Aaron Tinsley
Photos by Marla Carter and Beth Gwinn

This book is dedicated
to the memory of
Robert William Anderson Jr.
(Andy)

To Bob, Jo, Jeff, Laura and Matt

ANDY WOULDN'T LET ME

TABLE OF CONTENTS

AUTHOR'S NOTE

---Bryan---

When I first asked Christ to come into my
life at the age of 16, it changed my life. Despite
my failures and my letting Him down, I know
Christ is real and I know that His purpose for
coming into this world truly saved me. I am
surely not perfect, as none of us are, and my faith
shows me daily that I am a weak man.

Pastor Scotty Smith of Christ Community
Church in Franklin, Tennessee, shared this with
me one day regarding Paul. In 57 AD Paul said,
"I'm the least of the apostles" (1 Corinthians
15:9). Then, three years later in 60 AD he said,
"I'm less than the least of all God's people"
(Ephesians 3:8). Then, three years later in 63
AD, he said, "I'm chief of sinners" (1 Timothy
1:15). It seems the older Paul got, the more he
recognized his failures and his need for Christ. I
can identify. I understand the path of gaining
wisdom is not so much fun at times. And I
certainly understand how it humbles me.

I heard a song by Steve and Annie
Chapman soon after accepting Christ all those
years ago. I never wrote the lyrics down but I
remember them. And to this day I sing it
underneath my breath before taking the stage, or
when I feel like I have done something all by
myself.

If anyone sees any good thing in me
If anyone says that I'm somebody they'd like to
be
If they follow me before we go too far
Jesus I'll tell them that I am what You are
'Cause it would mean so much to me
If You're the only One they see
And if my life doesn't show them You
I know I'm living in vain
And if my life doesn't show them You
May they never know my name

 I have shared with my friend and co-writer of this book, Langdon Reid, how uncomfortable I am in discussing many things in this book. Many things that seem to place me in some sort of spotlight. It is my desire for you to receive the message of this book with extreme humility from me. Knowing Andy Anderson was a gift from God. His life and what he meant to everyone who came into contact with him far outweighs my stories in this book. It shows me all these years later that God's providence is amazing. I am forever blessed and changed due to this providence. Andy Anderson was and is a significant part of who I am in relation to others, as well as Christ.

 We are, as people seem to be, naturally drawn to the famous, the wealthy, the athletes, the actors, and entertainers. We find ourselves wanting to imitate them and for those of us that call ourselves Christians, when we do learn of a famous person that believes, we are quick to put them on a pedestal and look to them to be a great orator for Christ. After all, they have the spotlight, right?

Christ certainly uses all of His children. All of us. But it seems to me that Christ uses the weakest of men to empower His people. Andy Anderson was certainly not the best athlete I ever shared a locker room with; he was not the strongest athlete I ever shared a weight room with; he wasn't the fastest one to carry the ball; and I never saw him hit someone so hard that it took the breath out of them. But Andy Anderson was, by far, the toughest man I have ever known.

I will never be accused of being any sort of theologian. I don't know the correct title of those who study Angels, although I am certain I have heard the word before. Of course, I don't know whether or not you believe in angels, but with that said, when I look back at my life, I have to say that I definitely believe in them. And I truly believe Andy was a real angel, living and breathing, right next to me.

--- Bryan Kennedy

Chapter One

Go With Your Heart

···Langdon···
December 21, 2006 in Staunton, VA

I'm standing in the dark wing of the very stage in the very auditorium that I sat on 13 years ago on graduation night. My dad gave the "farewell and good luck" speech to a stage full of restless, anxious and undecided graduates. We, along with all the other college-bound kids across the country on that night, were officially being released into the world, to spread our wings and fly, in hopes of conquering challenges and making a better way for those behind us. I don't remember much about that night; however, I do remember being very hot and uncomfortable in that cheap impervious robe that was covering up a brand new navy blue double-breasted suit that obviously no one would ever see on this night because this polyester poncho reached all the way to the floor. It nearly covered the tassels on my loafers. And that mortarboard pressing down on my hair, this hair that I took an extra five minutes to comb because, after all, it was graduation, the most important night of my adolescent career thus far.

I do remember the prayer that Sarah, a dear and courageous classmate, gave to a packed auditorium. 1,135 to be exact. I closed my eyes and, even though the words she was saying were not necessarily registering in my brain, I remember thinking that this was the beginning of everything my parents, this school, and God had prepared me for. I had no idea what lay ahead, but I was sure that I would never again be on this stage, hot and uncomfortable, with a room full of eyes staring at me, looking for motivation or inspiration.

My mind drifted and wandered with thoughts of who would be at the graduation party and would I ever see any of these people again? Then my dad, who stood at a podium directed toward the audience, paused and turned around to address the 151 soon-to-be men and women sitting on metal folding chairs, of whom I sat among. He paused for a second longer than was comfortable, obviously to make sure he had everyone's attention. Then he said, "No matter what you do, go with your heart. You have to be true to yourself and the only way to do that is to go with your heart." Of everything I had learned in the past 18 years, this piece of wisdom surpassed it all.

So here I am, 31 years old, back in my home town of Staunton, Virginia, standing right inside the curtain of my high school alma mater. I'm wearing a bright orange camouflaged Santa Claus suit. These cheap plastic boots came with a pirate Halloween costume kit and the fur on this matching Santa hat is suffocating a long-forgotten haircut as sweat beads swim around the entire edge of the hat and my forehead. I'm hot and uncomfortable.

My cousin, Wil Reid, is sitting beside me, offstage, in one of those metal folding chairs, quite possibly the very same one I or he could have sat in for our graduations here. His happened two years earlier than mine, and his dad was the speaker at his graduation, also.

His Santa suit is not quite as obnoxious as mine, but definitely just as bright and eye-catching. It's a matching John Deere green pants and jacket boldly trimmed with canary yellow fur. Covering up his New Balance tennis shoes are two oversized felt "shoes" that curl completely on top with a bell at the end of each one. He's holding his sweat- drenched and worn out John Deere colored Santa hat in his hand, allowing his head to breathe for the first time since the show began. We give each other a quiet thumbs-up and our attention is directed back to center stage, where our other good friend and third thespian partner, Bryan Kennedy, is about to begin his soliloquy.

Bryan, too, is adorned, all six feet and four inches of him, in a pair of custom-made tri-colored high-top cowboy boots, a royal blue Santa suit with little Santas riding motorcycles, a black riding helmet with flames on either side and a pair of the thickest and ugliest goggles one has ever witnessed. This helmet and goggle pair is reminiscent of the hilarious Barney Fife "checkpoint chicky" look in the famous "Barney's Sidecar" episode of "The Andy Griffith Show." These outrageous and flamboyant suits make sense once you've seen the show, but for this particular scene, no one notices Bryan's suit···

just the meaning of the words that he is about to share with a captive audience.

Before he starts speaking to the audience, my mind starts to race with the timeline of how I got to be standing on this stage with Wil and Bryan performing this play and wearing these clothes.

I remember when Bryan attended college at Ole Miss to play football. Even though I was just a little guy and baseball was my sport, I've always watched football and kept up with it and knew that in order to play football at a top-notched well-respected SEC team like Ole Miss, you had to be pretty darn good. At the very least, Bryan was pretty darn good.

Our dads worked close in the music business, so therefore, I'd always heard about and known about Bryan. He lived in Nashville, Tennessee and I lived in Staunton, Virginia. I really got to know him in the early part of 2002, though. Wil, my music partner, and I signed with a record label and were in the process of finding songs for our debut album. Wil had come up with a title for a song, and it just begged to have Bryan's sense of humor all over it. We called him and told him the idea, and he was just as excited to write it with us as we were with him. Before the day was through, the three of us had written "She Don't Love Me More Than NASCAR" and it's been a favorite on that CD ever since. We'd write more songs together, but found ourselves sitting on his chocolate brown leather couches in

a cowboy-themed den staying up till the wee
hours of the morning talking about everything
under the sun. Every time Wil and I came to
town, we just stayed at Bryan's house; yes,
because it was free but mainly because we loved
those late night coffee talks. We entertained each
other equally, and a true friendship was born.

Then we got a call from Bryan one day
asking us if we'd consider being in a play. We
had never acted before but felt comfortable
enough in knowing how to work a stage that we
agreed. We were anxious to start rehearsing, but
Bryan told us that the play hadn't been written
yet.

So he commenced to writing and wrote a
Christmas play/show/musical titled *MistleToe
Roaster*. It's beautifully and cleverly written
about three friends, with the help of a campfire,
talking about the town's no-count hellion finding
Jesus and if we seek God just like the wise men
did in the Christmas story, your life's just going
to be a whole lot better. The cast of the entire
show is just the three characters (and
"characters" is meant in every capacity of its
definitions!) that are introduced to the audience
in the first ten minutes.

Wil's character is Big Daddy. Big Daddy is
a man of homespun intelligence with a left-field
approach on any issue that may arise. He is
dressed like a John Deere Santa Claus because
he is a tractor repairman and was playing Santa
for the kids' home Christmas party. I played the
character Hamlet, who is a laid-back country guy
searching desperately for the simpler way of life.
Hamlet just finished playing Santa at Wal-Mart

and headed straight to his tree stand to hunt; this is why his Santa suit is blaze orange camouflaged. Bryan plays the role of the lovable and laughable Chuck. To put it colloquially, Chuck is two steps ahead of a fit. Chuck has a record number of 49 girlfriends and his claim to fame is that he has appeared on the Jerry Springer Show. He has a unique and usually humorous way of seeing something in a very innocent and simple light. He is dressed like Santa Claus as he was invited by one of his numerous girlfriends to play Santa for a private party for one. We all three wound up on Christmas Eve on the backside of Hamlet's farm land around a campfire, or as it's known to the three characters, a toe roaster. I share all of this with you so you will better understand the entire experience the audience has been enjoying thus far. *MistleToe Roaster* has it all: stories, zaniness, original songs, traditional carols, laughs, wisdom, message, spirituality and downright heartfelt humility. The "heartfelt humility" part was about to take place.

As I mentioned earlier, every ear was hanging on to every word Bryan was delivering. And every heart was filling up with the right amount of humility needed to better understand God's world and how to live in it a little bit better. Bryan sat on the edge of the stage with his feet dangling over, his helmet and goggles in his hand and started to tell one of the more moving and touching stories to be told.

This was the scene:

(HAMLET AND BIG DADDY EXIT
STAGE LEFT TO HUNT FOR FIREWOOD.
CHUCK, ALONE, CENTER STAGE, BEGINS
REMINISCING ABOUT HIS 16TH BIRTHDAY)
CHUCK: *Well,*
who knew that July 27th
on my 16th birthday would
be my favorite Christmas
of all time.

> *See it all started*
when I was around 11
years old. It was just
before Christmas and I
was so excited. I'd been
looking through that J. C.
Penney catalog every
night for three months
trying to decide what to
ask for, for Christmas.
Mom and Dad always did
their best to get me and
my two sisters one big
present a piece. We each
made out a list, and we
usually got something
that was way down at the
bottom of the list, and
that was usually okay.

> *Well, this*
Christmas would be
different---I would make
sure of that. See, I had
my heart set on this
really cool bike! Oh, it
was the coolest bike ever

*made. It had the banana
seat, two silver reflectors
right underneath the seat
and about 18 spokes a
wheel so I could put
baseball cards in 'em to
give that perfect loud
rattle the faster I went. I
just had to have that
bike! And you know I was
11 years old, gettin' pretty
smart and all. I had
enough Christmases
behind me to know how to
"beat the system."
So, when I wrote out my
Christmas list that year, I
didn't write anything else
on that list except that
bike---the cool one on
page 127 in that J. C.
Penney catalog. See, I
knew this way I was sure
to get it.
        I handed the list to
my mom and she said,
"Chuck, baby you only
have one present on your
list." I smiled and said, "I
know." She went on to
explain to me that this
was not a good idea
because there was a good
possibility I wouldn't get
that bike, and that I*

*should list a few more
smaller things on my list.
I told her that I didn't
want anything else, and
that if I didn't get that
bike then I didn't want
anything....not anything
at all. She tried to talk me
into a longer list, but I
would have no part of
it...see, I knew how to get
that bike!*

*Well, along came
Christmas, finally! That
morning I woke up and
let me tell you I was the
most excited boy in the
world that Christmas
morning! I jumped out of
bed, ran toward the stairs
launching myself over the
first five or six without
touching them at all. I hit
the ground grabbing the
banister rail and slinging
myself around toward the
living room, sliding across
the floor nearly wiping
out the table mom had
left some cookies for
Santa on. Well, there I
was face to face with our
Christmas tree, my heart
pumping excitement and*

*adrenaline throughout my
entire 11 year old body!*

*But then a strange
feeling started coming
over me. My shoulders
raised and fell with my
heavy breathing, and my
eyes started blinking and
searching. My stomach
got sour and my knees
began to tingle a bit. I
was feeling sick way down
deep in my stomach. Then
my eyes explained to my
stomach. No bike. No
bike. Nowhere. I looked
all around the room and
still no bike. I turned
around and checked
behind me, one last hope
of Mom and Dad sneaking
in holding my new bike
and smiling! I turned and
there was Mom and Dad
but all I saw was the two
of them there crying.
Crying as if they were
saying they were sorry.*

*I tried to be big
about what was
happening, but I just
couldn't. See, my sisters
had already attacked the
tree and were ripping into
presents and screaming*

*and laughing and loving
every little gift they got.
And if things could get
worse, well... they did.
Not only did I not get the
bike I dreamed about, I
didn't get anything. I
didn't get one single
present. None at all.*

*I waited holding
back my tears and anger
while my sisters finished
opening all their presents,
and as soon as I could, I
went outside. I just
wanted to run, and run is
what I did. I took off as
fast as I could until I got
to our street. And then I
stopped, not really sure
where to go next.
Something caught my eye
down the road. I could see
it was my next-door
neighbor Steve. He was
riding his bike. But, as he
got closer, I could see a
huge smile on his face,
and it didn't take me long
to realize why he was
smiling: Steve was riding
a brand new bike. And
not just any brand new
bike; Steve was riding a
new bike just like the one*

on page 127! Just like the one I had asked for this Christmas!

He was so excited. But me, I was mad, jealous, and well...I took off running again. Back towards my house. No, I wasn't mad at Steve. He was my best friend and I felt terrible for running away 'cause I knew something was wrong with Steve. I heard my parents talking to Steve's parents one day about his disease. Something wrong with his brain. But I never noticed anything wrong with Steve. He was just fine to me. Heck he was smarter than me and made better grades than me and everything! But all I could think about at that time was me and that bike. It was an awful feeling, an awful Christmas! I didn't say Merry Christmas to Steve, I didn't say "I like your bike." I didn't say anything. I just ran back to the house, went inside and upstairs to my room and cried.

You know, that night my dad came into my room very late. He sat down on the edge of my bed. My face was buried in my pillow. He put his hand on my back and I heard him say, "I'm sorry son." And I thought, "You're sorry? You're sorry? I am the one that didn't get a bike for Christmas and you are sorry?"

After a moment I heard him take a deep breath and he whispered, "Chuck, someday son, you'll understand." I didn't want to hear that. I didn't want to hear anything from him. You know, if there was ever a day in my life that I could have hated my dad, it would have been that Christmas day.

Well, fast forward to July 27th on my 16th birthday. I came home from work that summer and walked into the kitchen and my dad

hollered, "Chuck, catch!"
And through the air flew
a set of car keys. I caught
'em but was confused.
Dad grabbed me by my
shoulder and led me out
into the garage. I turned
the corner and there she
sat. Dad had bought me
the most beautiful brand
new used car!

Oh, I ran around
to get in and Dad jumped
in the passenger side. I
put the key into the
ignition and was about to
crank her up when he
reached over and stopped
me. He said, "Hang on
Chuck, hang on just a
second." He asked me if I
remembered the
Christmas a few years
back when I had asked for
that bicycle. He asked me
if I remembered my list. I
told him I did. But why
in the world was he bring
this up right now? I didn't
care about that anymore.
Not really.

He went on to tell
me that he loved me more
than anything in the
world. It was a special

love, a love that only a father could feel for his only son. He told me that because he loved me so much, that when he saw my Christmas list, he decided he would do whatever it took to make my wish come true. He wanted nothing more than for me to have that bike.

I was listening, of course, but still very confused.

He continued on, telling me that after he saw my list, he went out and got an extra job working down at Sparks Jewelry so that he could afford to buy me that bike. And after he earned enough, he bought it. He bought me that bike!

I said, "You did?"

He said he was so proud when he picked that bike up that Christmas Eve and carried it over to the Ross' house late that night to put it together, all so he could surprise me the next morning. When he said that, it made me think of Steve Ross. You remember, the boy with the brain problem. My heart sank thinking of Steve 'cause he had just passed away a few days ago. His brain problem I learned was a tumor.

Dad was getting tears in his eyes and trying to hide them as he was telling me about that night how he and Mr. Ross were down in Steve's basement putting my bike together. Just about the time they were finished, they heard footsteps coming down the basement stairs, and they looked up and saw Steve. He had woken up and come down to see where his dad was. Dad said that when Steve saw the bike, his face lit up with a huge smile. He took off running toward the bike screaming, "Daddy, Daddy, Santa brought me a bike! He don't care that I'm sick! He don't care that I shouldn't ride a bike! Look Daddy! Santa brought me a brand new bike! Daddy look! Daddy look!" Dad said he ran to the bike and put his arms around it and hugged it like his best friend in the world. He hugged the bicycle. Dad couldn't hold back his tears now and neither could I.

Well, I knew what happened then. Dad said that he did what he knew he had to do. He gave Steve my bike. He said he left there and went back home and met Mom in the kitchen. He told her what happened and what he had done. They both knew it was the right thing to do, but they also both knew that it was 2 a.m. on Christmas Eve and the stores were all closed. And this also meant no presents for me, not a single one. He said they stood holding each other, crying in the kitchen.

He then told me, sitting in that car, that he was sorry, just the same way he said he was sorry that same Christmas, years ago, sitting on my bed. He told me back then that someday I would understand, and this was the day that understanding came.

See, my Dad didn't tell me how to love; he didn't say, "Chuck, here are the five best ways to love," or "Here is a book explaining how to love." No, he just showed me how to love. It may have taken five years, but he showed me.

He had something he loved very much: his only son, me. He knew that I wanted something and all he could do was think of how badly he wanted me to have it so he went and got an extra job and worked extra hours, sacrificing for me. And he did it. He got me what I wanted. And then what did he do? He gave it away. He gave it to someone that needed it more than me. Dad knew back then that Steve was dying. He knew the Ross' had bills---hospital, doctor

*bills---and he knew Steve
wasn't going to get much
that Christmas.
        Fathers. Isn't that
what they do? You know
like God the Father?
Loving us all the time.
And us, like little
children, wanting more,
thinking we need more
than we have. Us
thinking we deserve
more, asking for more. We
ask for things we don't
seem to ever get. You
know like me asking for
that bike and never
getting it.
God the father. He sees
the bigger picture, like
my dad did. I learned that
day to trust in both. My
dad and God. And that's
why July 27th on my 16th
birthday was my favorite
Christmas.*

The spotlight gleamed and focused on
Bryan's face, and it was as quiet and still in that
auditorium as it has ever been. About three
minutes into this scene, the audience knew that
this was something different than what they
were expecting. It was this way every night he
performed it. The people who had been laughing
all over themselves for the previous forty

minutes had no idea that they were about to be
slapped right in the heart with a story that not
only defines the meaning of Christmas, but is a
story for all to remember to help keep all
situations and the people we encounter daily in a
perspective that is brought to light with the
insight of this scene.

A few months after we had agreed to do
the play, Bryan was deep in to its inception. One
hot stuffy night, Wil and I were in Nashville
again for a few days, and after dinner with
Bryan, he wanted us to read through what he
had written thus far. Wil and I were perched on
one couch while Bryan, the Writer and Director
at this point, sat on the edge of another couch,
described scenes and prompted our characters as
to how they should act, talk and deliver each
line. We were rolling along, laughing, acting and
experimenting with each line, and at just the
first read-through, our confidence level was
rising a bit with each page of script. Then we got
to the bottom of page 31 and in italics it read
BIG DADDY. This was Wil's character and he
started reading aloud the lines of *well, who knew
that July 27th on my 16th birthday would be my
favorite Christmas of all time.* About a third the
way through, again about three minutes into it,
he and I shared a look with each other that there
was no silliness or zaniness or funny going on
with this scene. I put down my script and closed
my eyes, just to listen. Wil read through the
entire scene only to find tears settling in all three
of our eyes.

After a few more moments of silence to
digest what we had just heard, I asked Bryan

where he came up with the idea for this story. He offered that he had some help with it. "I felt lead and inspired by a friend of mine back in high school, Andy Anderson. He meant a lot to me, but I didn't realize it then. I guess it just came to surface for this play."

Wil admitted the power and message in the story and introduced the idea that it's going to be a hard one to deliver, staring at all those faces, night after night. Bryan admitted that that is why he had written this scene for another character, because he had already realized that he may not be able to get through it each night.

Bryan continued to write and finish the play. He'd send us updates and things to rehearse and think about, but it wasn't till we all three got back together for our first official read-through, that when we came to the *Steve's Bike* scene, the character in italics before it read *CHUCK*, Bryan's character. He told us that this scene had been laying heavy on his mind and even heavier on his heart, and he felt the right thing to do was to have his character deliver the story. The obvious was not lost in this decision. This is something that not just Chuck needed to tell, but Bryan Kennedy needed to tell.

Every night he tells this story it takes on a deeper meaning.

The crowd is fixed on Bryan. No one is moving, not physically. Just spiritually. I hear a baby start crying. This breaks the silence which has us all entrapped. However, it won't be until

this scene is finished and intermission begins,
that our thoughts and feelings will be able to
shift back to normal.

I look over at Wil and realize that I have
known him my entire life and have known that
he has always been comfortable and at his best
on a stage. And I know how I came to be dressed
in this silly Santa suit four days before
Christmas in my hometown performing this play-
--I went with my heart. But how did Bryan get
here? This tall good-looking frame of a man with
steely eyes and a soul so old-fashioned it was
obviously made three generations ago. One of the
most sought-after football talents in the late 70's-
--a talent that could have played anywhere he
wanted. Then his talents turned to music and his
name on songs that have sold over 100 million
records. This Bryan Kennedy. How in the world
did he get to be standing on this stage here
tonight?

Chapter Two

Ok Bryan, Go Get It

---Bryan---

I don't know how I came to be standing on the stage that night. I can tell you this though: I hated doing the *Steve's Bike* scene. Every night. Hated it. I loved everything about that play; working with Wil and Langdon, the rehearsals, the music, the laughs, the traveling, the people, the different theaters, the overall message of the play. But I hated doing that scene.

Looking back, the reason I hated doing that scene was because it was too close to me. I cried when I wrote it, I cried when I rehearsed it, and I cried every night I performed it. It took me to a place that I wasn't ready to go back to. It reminded me of a time and a place in my life that wasn't all bad on the surface but wasn't very good at all deep down. It stirred those very feelings inside of me that I wasn't ready to revisit. I felt as if I had a black eye on my conscience that never completely healed and reciting the lines to *Steve's Bike* revealed this black eye again.

And also, I wasn't meant to be standing on a stage dressed like a wayward bent Santa Claus plucking heartstrings for sport every night. I'm a football player. A 6'4" hard-hitting defensive end who knew he was not the biggest

or meanest to play this game, but was just scared
enough to play the game hard and mentally
tough enough to dare you to try to knock me off
the ball or get around my side. I was plenty used
to the taste of my own blood in my mouth;
certainly not the salt from my own tears every
night.

    I grew up on a dead end street. I think
today they call them cul-de-sacs. I am the middle
boy of three---Gordon, my older brother by a year
and five months, and my younger brother Shelby
by a year and four months. Our dead end street
was surrounded by four houses and out of each
house came boys, all very close to the same age.
There were seven or eight of us. This made for
the most wonderful dead end street in the world.
We spent all of our time outside; all day and
most of the night till bedtime.
    All of us boys had several things in
common and I would say the most predominant
thing in our lives was this something that still
serves as some sort of 'life teacher' to me. A word
that both provokes me and demands my
attention: Football. I feel that when someone
says this word, there is no way it could sound the
same as it does to me. Football. The same way an
old song might resurrect a place in your life or
the whiff of a certain perfume a long time ago
makes your soul tingle, the word football just
does something to me.
    There were not only days of playing
football with Scott, Randy, Hal, Butch, Rick,

Gordon and Shelby, and others from time to time, but there were years of playing football. We didn't know there was such a thing as a 'football season.' We played football all year long. In fact, I don't even think I knew what a basketball was. I know I didn't bounce one or shoot one until I was eleven years old. From my earliest memories, beginning at three or four years old, all I can remember is running with that football in my arm, dodging trees, dodging my friends and brothers across the street. I can really feel myself running with that ball, getting gang tackled, and being underneath piles of bodies, grass stains on my knees, and the dirt in my mouth and on my clothes! I never tired of playing football.

It didn't matter what the weather was either. If it was hot in the summer, we never seemed to notice, if it were freezing or snowing, we just wore extra socks on our feet and on our hands. No weather could keep us from playing football. In fact, the worse the weather, the heavier the rain and the muddier the turf, the more fun football was.

One of my most vivid memories of this time in my life was attempting to watch football on T.V. Gordon, Shelby and I would be inside around a fire Dad had built. We were more likely to be inside a bit more on very cold days. He would want us to watch a NFL playoff game on T.V. with him and we were all about it, too. We had our favorite players and our favorite uniforms. We also had football cards we were lucky enough to get from time to time. We had our electric football teams that we would paint to

represent our favorite teams. We'd gather in the
den to watch the kick-off. However, the idea of
the three of us being inside and only *watching*
football lasted only a few series of downs. I don't
believe we would ever make it to the end of the
first quarter. All watching football seemed to do
was stoke the fire in all of us to go outside to *play*
football. And it seemed to have the same effect on
all of us living on the dead end! We never called a
neighbor to ask if he wanted to go outside and
play---we'd all show up outside at the same time.
So, I don't remember the first entire football
game I ever saw, but I am pretty sure it was
probably the first one I ever played in a few
years later in the third grade.

But a few years before this was when I
celebrated my most memorable Christmas. I was
about five years old, and my brothers and me
came downstairs that morning to find an orange
rubber kicking tee sitting under the tree. My
heart went to my knees as the blood rushed to
my head and I rushed to the tree. I picked it up
and smelled it. Just like I had imagined. I had
seen them on TV in the real games but had never
seen one in person. It had three prongs on the
bottom and two on the top. I couldn't believe I
had a real professional tee, just like the real
kickers used in the real NFL. And I was so happy
that Santa liked football, too! He knew exactly
what to bring me that Christmas to make me the
happiest kid in the world.

I didn't think that my love for football
could be elevated any higher, but this orange
funny shaped piece of rubber did just that. It was
a big hit in the neighborhood---now we could kick

off! And though I loved to kick the ball, what I
really found myself loving to do was to return the
kicks! I loved to run with the ball. And run I did.
Looking back I would have to credit those days
as to why I became the football player I
ultimately came to be. Dodging trees and my
friends with a football in my arm became second
nature. It was as natural as tying my shoes,
writing my name, or eating a bowl of cereal for
breakfast. I wasn't a part of football; it was a
part of me. So it's fair to say that at an early age,
I quickly recognized and somehow understood
exactly how much this sacred sport meant to me.

Another inkling of this happened on an
average day in the neighborhood when I was
across the street at Scott Culbertson's house. It
was his birthday, and he came out to show us
what his dad had gotten him for his birthday. He
was so excited and couldn't wait to show his
buddies. The door opened and all I could see was
red! Scott was holding a pair of red football
shoulder pads! I stood there on his front porch
and watched as Scott slid those shoulder pads
over his head. I could feel the anger or jealousy
or something building inside me. As his head
popped through the opening in the middle, a
smile crossed his face, and I found something
cross my face as well: tears. I wanted shoulder
pads! I wanted to play football. I was the one
that should have the shoulder pads! I was the
one that should be playing football!

This desire, this quest, this destiny never
left me even though we moved from that dead
end road when I was in the middle of my second
grade year. We moved to a place where it took

some getting use to. Honestly, I never got use to it. We moved to a house with no neighborhood; therefore, no neighbors; therefore no more backyard football games. It was like living on an island. This was a very dramatic change in my life and I remember the empty feeling all those days not playing football in our new house as much as the great memories of playing all those days on the dead end street. I don't remember much more about my life at that time at all outside of football. It seems my memories as a young child and really through most of my youth, revolved around and were connected to football.

It's obvious by now that my formative years were hinged solely on the idea of playing, watching and loving football to its utmost. I can tell you where I bought my first cleats, what that first mouthpiece tasted like, and what color *my* first set of shoulder pads were. My first organized team I played on was the Percy Priest Tigers and my jersey number was 48. I can't remember what I had for dinner last night or some family member birthdays, but I remember what was important to me.

Another major incentive that I remember, perhaps as vividly as any experience I have ever had in athletics, was something that happened often in practice my third grade year. Something that seemed to feed the future in me. Something that seemed to encourage me in some way. Something that said to me, this is you. This is what you are, what you are good at, what you are destined to do or to become.

It would always be the end of practice. Mike Johnson was our coach. We didn't call our

coach, Coach or Coach Mike back in those days.
Coaches were called by their first names. Mike
was my coach. Mike would call the entire team
up to gather around him. He took a football and
threw it down to the opposite end of the practice
yard about forty yards or so. He would let the
ball come to a rest. Then, like Labrador
retrievers, we would all stare intently on the
football. Waiting for our command to retrieve.
He'd say, "When I blow the whistle I want to see
which of you is tough enough to run down there
and bring the ball back to me." I remember the
excitement of this test and being locked in on
that ball. Picturing myself running and grabbing
it before anyone could get to it, then running
back while the others tried to tackle me and take
the ball from me. I was made for this! I wanted
that ball and I wanted to be the one to bring it
back to Mike.

One day was different from the rest,
though. Mike blew his whistle, and everyone
bolted like frightened horses. Like all the others,
I bolted from my relaxed position towards the
waiting football. I had not been in the ideal
position to start this drill; there were several
boys in front of me who would no doubt get an
unfair head start. A slight obstacle, but one I
knew I could overcome. And just as this thought
was being processed in my mind and my cleats
began to dig into the grass, I felt my body being
jerked to a stop! I felt like I was being clothes-
lined from behind. Mike had reached his hand
out and grabbed the inside collar of my shoulder
pads. His fingers underneath my collar were
deliberately holding me back from running with

the others. I was staring at my teammates who
were just about to reach the football. I looked
over my shoulder through my facemask at Mike.
He could read my face; he could read my question
without me asking. He quietly said, "Just wait,"
as he watched the pile form down the yard.
Somehow I trusted that there was some sort of
reason for this. I turned my focus back to the
huge pile now engulfing a football smothered
somewhere underneath the helmets, shoulder
pads, and cleats. I bit into my mouthpiece,
reminiscent of a ravenous stray dog. Then
suddenly I felt the tension being released from
Mike's grip and I heard these words, again,
spoken very softly, "Ok, Bryan. Go get it."

I turned for a short moment to look at
Mike, just long enough to get approval. And it
came in the form of a smile. I took off running
toward the pile and dove into the mass of
players. I fought, dug, and wrestled with the
other arms and legs and hands until I clinched
that ball to my side. I somehow got to my feet
with the ball while the others were trying to
tackle me all the while running back to Mike.
Running, hard and fast, waiting for someone to
grab me from behind, but somehow knowing they
wouldn't, they couldn't. Just like the dead end
street days.

Mike would repeat this drill once a week
and sometimes two or three times in a row on the
same day. It became routine. I would just wait
until he blew the whistle and I heard, "Ok,
Bryan. Go get it." I never came back to Mike
without the ball. I would race back to him and
toss him the ball like it was no big deal. Was it a

big deal? To this day, I don't know. Nor do I
know how I did that. I guess you could say I
wanted that football more than anyone else. I
wanted it so bad I would fight for it, and it meant
so much to me to get it!

The word Football was more than a word,
more than an object, more than a game. Football
was me. It was my desire, my focus and my
entire world. It defined me; it gave me my reason
to live.

And yet, it would become something I
would desperately want to quit. But Andy
wouldn't let me.

Chapter Three

His Reason, Our Purpose

···Langdon···
December 21, 2006 in Staunton, VA

Standing on the side of this stage, my eyes go back and forth between my two "brothers", Wil and Bryan. Over the last three months of performing and traveling together, I've learned so much about these two men that have made me a better person for it. Every time I meet somebody new, I can't help but to think how this person could or is going to ultimately affect my life to some degree. But it's those that I've known my entire life that I quickly overlook. Any skeletons in my closet or secrets buried deep, these two guys know about them.

And just like during a long pulpit prayer, my mind wanders, only this time in a deeper direction. I notice how quiet the audience is. They realize now that this scene, *Steve's Bike*, is not going to make them laugh, but that Bryan is taking them somewhere they weren't expecting to go tonight. I can't help but to wonder *what is God up to?* Silly me, I'll never completely know. But it never hurts to ask. And I find a familiar comfort in my own beliefs.

I'm a believer in that all things happen for a reason. At the risk of speaking for the rest of

*the Christian world, I'm pretty sure all of us
believe in this to a certain extent, too. Maybe
you've never actually thought about it before or
this idea has just been termed another way.
Preachers, scholars, and students of seminary
may use words like Almighty, Sovereign,
Predestination, Foreknowledge, and
Omnipotence. It all depends on the denomination
and the choice of the path to our own salvation.
But basically, if we believe in God and ultimately
subscribe to the notion that He is the sole Author
of life as we know it, then it's only natural to
accept that God has a reason and a purpose for
each one of us. Great or small. Revealed or
hidden. Understood or simply accepted. I believe
I happened for a reason. And I believe you
happened for a reason. He took His time to
create us so we are here to fulfill a purpose. The
purpose. Our purpose. His reason.*

Chapter Four

Linemen over there, backs over here!

---Bryan---

My fourth grade football season was very successful, losing only one game. My fifth grade year proved a bit better going undefeated, and my sixth grade year almost as successful. We were undefeated during the regular season and ended it playing in an All Star game for the final game of the year. I guess our team was thought good enough to be an All Star team of sorts because the league took the best talent of all the other teams and slated those athletes against our team. We were evidently not *that* good, though. We got beat pretty handily that night.

The All Star game finally ended, and I was not happy. I got killed every time I touched the ball. I remember thinking, *let Bob run it. They are all waiting for me to carry it.* Bob Dale, the other tail back, a great runner. Number 22. I wish they had let Bob run it more. We might have won that night and I wanted to win. Let me put it this way: it's not so much that I loved to win, it's that I hated to lose. If there is an ounce of competitiveness in you and you have a passion for something, then you know exactly what I'm talking about. I felt dejected and down.

Both teams gathered around midfield on the press box side of the field. I remember 'hitting a knee', a term I still seem to respond to automatically if the phrase comes to mind or my ears. Carter Brown, my coach, one of the greatest I ever had, was gathering us together. I remember thinking I would never play for Carter again. This really bothered me. The announcer over the loud speaker awarded both teams their appropriately ranked trophies.

I was hoping for all of this to be over and done with when he announced the MVP award. Still lost in my own thoughts, I heard a voice somewhere behind me say, "Bryan go get it. You got MVP." I froze, still down on one knee; not really sure why I'm getting this trophy when I was gang-tackled for the last 30 minutes and was on the losing team. And I didn't even know what MVP stood for. I could see a man---a man I had seen before---standing less than six feet from me. He was a man that looked like he might have had a better place to be or at least on this night he might have been forced to do something he didn't really want to do. But later I would learn that this was simply his look. It was a very intense look; one that communicated with not much need for words. It was the look of Coach Carlton Flatt, the head football Coach at Brentwood Academy. He just stood there soaking in his stoic self, his lips pinched together as if to say, "Son, did you not hear your name? Now get up here and get this thing!"

I rose to both feet while others were clapping and a very uncomfortable feeling came over me walking to this man. The man held his hand out for me to shake and with the other, he handed me the evidently ever-coveted MVP trophy. He didn't say a word to me. Oh, but he said so much.

It was in his face, in his eyes. I could tell even as a young boy, this man, this Coach, was not much on trophies and not much on singling out players as "better" or "more valuable" than the rest of the team. I sensed that right away from him, and truthfully, I agreed. I could see all of this in his face---that face that I would soon find myself staring into thousands of times on the field---but more importantly, thousands of times off the field.

All I could think about as a twelve year old boy, no longer having any neighbors and finding myself pretty bored after school, was playing football. Only now I turned my thoughts to playing football at Brentwood Academy, just like my older brother, Gordon, was doing. But first I had to be accepted to the school and that meant taking a test. Something I was never very good at. But if I wanted to play more football and play for that man and his "look", then I had to take it.

The letter finally came and my mom told me I had been accepted. She had to be the one to tell me because the nerves inside of me wouldn't allow me to read it. Nervous was now gone and excitement set in. Perhaps excited for the wrong reasons, though. I never considered "going to school" at Brentwood Academy. I never considered that it was extremely revered academically. Heck, to be honest, I wasn't quite sure what the word academic meant! (Now you understand why I was nervous about taking the test.) The only thing I considered was that it was a place to play football *while* I went to school. I only saw the world as a place to play football.

My first day of 7th and 8th grade football practice at Brentwood Academy marked the specific day a 'word seed' was planted in my spirit. By a 'word seed' I mean I knew the word and its meaning, but when it came to football there was no way this word would take root and grow. But, on my first day of football practice at Brentwood Academy, the seed took. And it began to grow like an angry weed.

A lot of things were very different about this practice from all the other practices I had. But the main question on my mind was *where was Coach Flatt? The guy with "the look?" Where was the coach that handed me the trophy?* He was nowhere to be seen. The man who was obviously going to be my coach blew a whistle. I knew that meant it was time to start whatever you do at the start of a Jr. High football practice. We all, like little sheep being corralled by a border collie, stampeded toward the man with the whistle. Just like the first page of every manual on *How To Be a Coach*, he started barking orders at a fast and demanding pace and shouting at us to *move, move, move!* The orders were then, "Lineman over there, backs over here! Lineman over there, backs over here with me!"

For clarification for those of you who are not familiar with football lingo, "linemen" are the players you see on the line of scrimmage, along side the ball, or those down in a stance in front of the quarterback or all of those big guys that are squatted leaning forward on one arm. Linemen are the ones that block for the guys behind them.

And those guys behind the linemen are the
"backs." The backs are the guys that carry the
football. In other words, the linemen usually get
no recognition for their work and the backs get
all the recognition for not only their work but
also the linemen's work.

Over and over, this man spat these orders
out of his mouth and, like mice in a dark room
when someone turns on the lights, little shoulder
pads and bigger shoulder pads dispersed in the
two different directions. I heard the order, and I
was quick to be one of the first to stand near this
new coach who had called for the backs to stay
with him.

I had only come to a rest for maybe a full
second, anxiously awaiting what was to happen
next to a back at a Brentwood Academy football
practice when this coach says to me, as he turns
my shoulders and shoves me away, "You're too
big to be a back. You go with the linemen."

Humiliation, dejection and downright
hurt do not begin to describe the feeling down
deep inside of my stomach. In one quick turn of a
coach's order, I was stripped of who I was. I was
a back. I wasn't just a back, I was the MVP back,
right? Which, I guess, meant that I was the best
back in the city, right? I can't remember if I was
more disappointed or confused. In all my years of
playing football, I encountered the wrong end of
a concussion at least three times. I can honestly
say that without being touched, hearing these
words, no doubt, was the hardest I'd ever been
hit.

Many of you may think that what I am
about to say is foolish, childish, silly, or at the

very least, petty. But this one single moment
brings tears to my eyes to this day. That feeling
of falling off the highest cliff and you keep on
falling and falling. I found my legs moving
toward the linemen, and my heart moving away
from football. The one thing I loved. The one
thing I was good at. The one thing I felt that was
my gift. Just give me the ball and I'll run for you
all day long. I'll score more touchdowns than
Walter Peyton. It was what I was made to do.
But there was no turning back.

Thankfully, I am much too mature and
forgiving today because back then, this was my
first taste of some sort of hate. I jogged over to
this group I did not and could not belong in. I
joined the linemen. And I hated it. I hated
practice. I hated the Coach. I hated football.

I was too young to speak up for myself, to
go see someone, or tell my dad or mom. I didn't
know what to do. I just went along with it. Then,
after maybe the first week of practice, something
happened to me for the first time in my football
career. Someone fell on the outside of my knee,
bending it in places it doesn't bend. Those three
loud pops are imbedded in my ears and mind.
The pops were minor compared to the incredible
pain that ensued immediately after the last ring
of the last pop. The tears of this pain hit the
ground right before my entire body crumbled on
the field.

I was on crutches the entire season.
Unfortunately, this would not be the last time I
heard the pops, and it would most certainly not
be the last time I did time with crutches. But it

was perhaps the worst time. Not the worst injury I ever experienced, but the worst timing for one.

I was in a new school. I was trying to make new friends. I was trying to find my way around in this new environment. It was so easy the day before I went with the linemen. I knew who I was before that day. I was Bryan Kennedy, the football player. I was Bryan, the running back. I was the one you couldn't catch, the one you couldn't outrun, and the one you couldn't tackle. And now I was a lineman, and a lineman with a torn-up knee who couldn't play.

This changed my whole world and changed it dramatically. I look back on it now and know I was depressed. First, I didn't know how to be a lineman. Then I didn't know how to be this kid on crutches. I didn't know how to make a friend without being a running back football player. I was always the kid that people made friends with because of who I was; the football player. He was gone. I was lost in this new world, depressed and miserable. Those feelings of wanting to quit had never been stronger. But again, little did I know, that Andy wouldn't let me.

Chapter Five

Identity Theft

···Langdon···
December 21, 2006 in Staunton, VA

As I peer around the curtain to catch a glimpse of the audience, my right hand reaches for the right side of my elastic belt. It's just a cheap belt I picked up somewhere to wear underneath this bright orange camouflaged St. Nick style parka. It has two purposes: one, to keep my baggy Santa pants up. Two, it holds my wireless battery pack for my microphone. Whenever I'm not on stage in a scene, I am constantly reaching under my coat and pushing the little slide power button to the left, the OFF position. By constantly, I mean about every 45 seconds or less. Yes, it's a nervous and compulsive habit I've developed but for good reason. I'm always concerned that somehow, someway, some thing has kicked this button accidentally to the ON position, and I'm going to say something incriminating or embarrassing "off stage." It hasn't happened yet, but my fears are good caution.

I started this nervous habit with my wallet and cell phone. I wear my phone the same place on my belt as the battery pack and throughout the day, find myself checking to make sure it's still hanging on. And my wallet is in my back pocket. So with one quick undetectable motion, I can feel for both and know that my essentials are intact. Lack of good caution led to this fear of them not being where they should be. I've had both of them stolen a couple of times in my life, and an unexplainable emptiness settled in immediately. My temples got hot and my Adam's apple started to swell. My mind went blank and finally came back to asking *why would someone steal what's most important to me?* I understand that most steal for money, but leave the cards, pictures and memberships. They don't need those!

My wallet and phone are a part of me and who I am. My phone is my calendar and holds appointments and phone numbers and quick voice recordings and daily notes of reminders. These couple of robbers stripped me clean. They didn't just pick my pocket, they chipped a piece of me.

So I've gotten my wallet and phone stolen, and Bryan has been instructed not to be a running back. These may seem like entirely two different things, but they're not. Both are forms of identity theft. Both are examples of how a quick unsuspected moment can change our views toward people and how we continue to live our lives. It's the butterfly effect: the mere flutter of a butterfly's wings can alter our lives as we know it. We can become cynical, hardened and untrusting of others due to the action of one. And this simple act of caution we are forced to take can easily meld into a fear. And fear into unhappiness.

At first glance, it sounds so petty. But an avalanche is started with just a snowflake. We must remind ourselves that even though God is on His own time, He is still on our side. We just have to make sure that we are on His.

It takes time. Time filled with struggles and faith. And still always knowing that all things do happen for a reason.

Chapter Six

A Miracle Coach

···Bryan···

I never played a down my 7th grade football season, I just wore my jersey on Fridays and stood around on crutches. My 8th grade year was much different. I was once again a lineman but a lineman that hadn't lost his natural knack for this game of football. Defensive tackle was my new position, along with being an offensive tackle. Offensive tackle? Me? I used to be the one carrying the football into the end zone, and now I'm blocking and making the way for others to climb up my back so they can score the six points. Still to this day, it is hard for me to say this.

By this stage in my life I knew that hitting people was a way of taking out my frustration. Frustration that came from home, school, choices, and just the overall frustrations that came with living through those awkward early teen years. I hate the phrase "trying to find myself," but in actuality, I guess that describes it best.

We played a bowl game down in Lawrenceburg, Tennessee. I went out before the game as a team captain for the coin toss. One of the other team captains glared at me and said, "We're coming right at you. We're coming right

over you!" I assume this was to scare me or
intimidate me. This was the first day I realized
that, even though I hated being a lineman, I
loved the idea of someone thinking they were
going to run over me. I loved the challenge and
accepted it with excitement and some more
frustration. They came right at me, but they
didn't go right over me. In fact, I don't remember
them running to my side much the rest of the
game. I thought *why would someone say that to
another player? You're just going to make him
mad.* And did it ever. Boy, it made me mad. And
I took it out on everyone I could hit in a different
colored jersey than mine. I never communicated
using words: only actions. I never told anybody
how knots in my stomach twisted tighter
together because I was dealing with issues and
questions off the field. But on the field, I just put
on some pads and knocked the devil out of some
other innocent opponent who signed up to play
the game. It's the only thing I knew. And it was
what I knew to work.

Remember the guy that I wanted to play
for in the 7th grade? The coach---the one with the
steely eyes, the pinched lips holding my MVP
trophy? The one with that unexplainable and
unforgettable look? Coach Carlton Flatt. In the
spring of my 8th grade year, he suggested that I
participate in spring football practice with the
varsity. In other words, I'd be a 14-year-old boy
practicing with 15-18 year olds. The gesture on
his part made me feel important. It was his way
of saying, "I think you're good, or at least you
have the potential to be really, really good. And I
think playing with talent older and stronger will

only make you better." Yes, it did make me feel special; however, it didn't sound like much fun to me. I would be the youngest lineman on the team and the skinniest! But I went along. Not because I wanted to, but because I hadn't worked up enough nerve to quit, yet.

I broke both of my thumbs that spring and looking back, I can see now that was a blessing since that was the worse physical injury I incurred. But the mental injury was much greater. I had already fallen out of sorts with my identity and had now fallen out of love with, my only love, football. Everyday I got my brains beat in by seniors. What was supposed to be making me stronger seemed to be only making me weaker. It made me want to separate myself from the very sport I once coveted. If they would only do things my way. If they would only put me back in the backfield! If they would only let me put that ball under my arm and let me run with it! I could dodge and get past these Neanderthals that were smashing me senseless down after down! If I could just run past them and feel that thrill once again! If they would just let me catch it or kick it off the tee! Did they not know that I could do these things better than most? I never got the chance to show them. I was a lineman. I was just a beat up 14-year-old tall, lanky and skinny lineman. A kid with no neighbors, no direction, no incentive and no desire to do anything. That included having no desire to be me---whoever *me* was.

The week before two-a-day practices
started, the summer of my freshman year, my
"word seed" was ready to harvest. I picked up the
phone and called Coach Flatt. Nervous doesn't
even come close to what my head, hands and
heart were feeling. I couldn't tell if I was
sweating or the tears had backed up in my
forehead and now coming through every pore I
had. Nonetheless, it had to be done. I had to put
this "quit" word in the barn. No one knew I was
making this call---not my friends, brothers, dad
or mom. Coach answered the phone on the first
ring; not even enough time to let me hang up and
back out. My adolescent voice quivered, "Coach
Flatt, this is Bryan Kennedy and I am quitting
football this year."

Even as I type that phrase, I get that
same lump in my throat as when I first uttered
this phrase. I had so much respect for this man
and this game, I didn't want to let either one of
them down. Still, the one thing that had once
made me happy was now the main thing in my
life I had come to hate. The one thing that gave
me purpose and showcased a gift that I had---
running the football---had been switched
drastically to the grueling demands of the line of
scrimmage---a lineman. I didn't necessarily want
revenge for those who put me in this new
position; I just wanted to be done with it. Done
with it all. No more football.

I remember the silence on the other end of
the phone. He cleared his throat and began to
calm himself down. It was obvious he was
shocked, and it was obvious he was mad.

I don't know how he did it but he talked me into showing up for two-a-day practices and playing that season. I hated it. I never hated him; just hated being a lineman. As a youth, you are really stuck with coaches. You have no choice. There are good ones, bad ones and ones that are okay. It is a blessing when you have a good one and a miracle to have a great one. I had more miracles than good ones and only a few rotten ones. Coach Flatt was a miracle. He was more of a surrogate father to me. My respect for him at that time was not something a 14-year-old boy would recognize. I was not the best student in the school. I didn't take to history, science, English, and certainly not math and algebra. Coach Flatt would meet with me in the locker room every day for 45 minutes to teach me algebra. Me, Coach and that Cross pen of his; all three solving for X. I never got it, but he never quit trying to teach me. This didn't happen for just a season; it happened on and off for six years. He wouldn't give up on me. He pushed and pushed and pushed. I will forever love him for that. Didn't care for it much then, but I appreciate it so much today. All for a reason.

It was the last regular season game of my freshman year. I hadn't played a down the entire season. This night, like all the other game nights, I found myself moving around on the sideline to stay loose or, on this particular night, to stay warm. I was never a talker--- I just stayed to myself mostly. I was always the last one to run through the banner at the beginning of the game.

Keep in mind, I hated playing but so far my
talent was the only thread keeping me attached
to it. So my main concern this night was to stay
warm, and the last thing on my mind was
actually playing.

It was into the fourth quarter, and the
game was on the line. There was a blanket of fog
or haze surrounding the field. My fourteen year-
old mind was deep into wandering *what exactly
is fog and what causes it?*

"Kennedy!" somebody shouted. My brain
first told me it was a call for my older brother,
Gordon. But he was already in.

"Kennedy! Where the flip is Kennedy?"
Players were grabbing at me, pulling my jersey
towards the origin of my name being called. I
reached up with both hands to button my
chinstraps on each side of my helmet. I knew
they were already fastened, but still my fingers
tried to fasten them somehow tighter. It was a
nervous habit or maybe just a gesture to make
sure I was as prepared as I could be. I was
breathing hard as if I had been playing the full
game. I ran now through a maze of teammates
who, I'm sure, were just as surprised to hear my
name being called as I was. I was approaching
the voice shouting my name, a little louder and
madder each time. Coach Flatt grabbed my
jersey and slung me with all his might onto the
playing field. "You get in there and get that
flippin' quarterback!"

I sprinted to the huddle. I don't know who
came out or why. I looked around the huddle,
and all I saw were a bunch of juniors and seniors
that, it seemed, I was seeing for the first time

ever. They had a different look in their eyes. No doubt, it was frightening. Did I look like that to them? My mind was racing. They were sweating, bloody, panting, and all quiet waiting for the defense to be called. It was as if I had been parachuted into the middle of a battle. A battle where my side needed another soldier but when I showed up in the huddle with a sparkling clean uniform, well, I don't think I did much for my team's confidence toward outcome of the battle.

The captain of our team grabbed my facemask and as he yelled at me, sweat and spit served as the appetizer to the words that followed. "You get to the quarterback! You hear me? Get to the quarterback!" We broke the huddle with a clap, and there I was getting in my three-point stance. The ball was snapped, and the next thing I knew, like a pit bull chasing a t-bone, I chased that quarterback down in the backfield. I didn't sack him, but I hit him. I hit him just as he released the ball. When he got up off the ground, he had a look of his own. A look that asked *who are you and where did you come from?* Again, that same look on the next play and on the next.

It was all over before I knew it. We won the game, and I had proved myself to Coach Flatt and the entire varsity squad. But I still hadn't proved anything to myself.

I had two best friends all through high school: Wally Knox and John Patton. Wally was a running back and John was a quarterback. I guess if I couldn't be a back, I could at least be friends with them. True friends they were.

Because of entangling home life issues, unhappiness at school, compounded with the overall idea of not knowing exactly who I was or even wanted to be, my hate for playing football only intensified. I had loved this sport so much when I would carry that oblong ball all over the field dodging and hurdling opponents and diving into end zones. But now that I was no longer a running back, I felt like my final layer of comfort and happiness had been stripped as well. I had friends on the team, and my level of play was only getting better and stronger, but the love for it deflated to just a speck in my heart. There was a constant struggle way down deep, and I had to get rid of it. The only way to do that was to quit.

I told Wally during study hall the first day spring practice was to begin that I was going to quit football. Because he was a great friend, he did what great friends do: he laughed at me. Wally thought I was all talk. As good of friends as we were, even he didn't know the feelings for the game that had swelled inside of me.

I stood outside the coaches' office door after the last period bell rang. I saw my right hand go up in front of me as I watched my knuckles knock against the wooden door. It was only seconds before it opened. Behind it stood my basketball coach, Rick Miller, (another miracle coach), all 6'7" of him. "What do you want?"

I replied sternly, "I am here to talk to Coach Flatt."

"What about?"

"I am going to quit football." He, too, broke into laughter, just like Wally had. He opened the door wider as if to say come on in. "He'll be here in a minute."

I sat down on a small couch. I didn't speak to Coach Miller, I didn't want to. He made me mad, too, just like Wally had. Now I was even more determined. I could hear noises outside the door and every time, I anticipated Coach Flatt opening the door. It was painful and stressful. The sitting and waiting, knowing what I was about to do: to face a dragon that everyone thought I couldn't slay. Their laughing told me so.

The door suddenly flew open and Coach Flatt walked in with both arms full of books. He had a relaxed look on his face until he saw me sitting there. He didn't speak to me; he addressed Coach Miller as if I were not even within earshot. "Kennedy. What's he doing here?"

Coach Miller found his grin again. "He says he wants to quit football."

The books Coach Flatt was carrying in his arms hit his desk like a sledgehammer against a rock. His eyes narrowed, his lips began to withdraw inward from his profile. He stared at the books he just slammed. He began to rub the top of his head clockwise with the palm of his hand. He rolled his chair over in front of me and sat down inches from my face. It was show time and it was on!

He stared at me and I back at him. We locked pupils. I had to make sure I didn't blink. If I broke eye contact, he would win. We sat there for twenty minutes but it seemed more like 14 years. He bombarded me with questions and reasons. I stayed true to my mission in going in there. I wouldn't back down. And neither would he.

I did not want to be a lineman anymore, and this was my hour to liberate myself from football forever.

An hour later I walked out of that office. I went straight to the locker room and dressed in full pads. The sinking feeling in my stomach was due to the fact that I even failed at quitting. I felt lower than low and I had no idea why I was getting dressed and heading back out to the field. As I made my way out, I heard laughter in the distance, and I knew who it belonged to. As I stepped on to the practice field, the first person I saw was the first person who saw me not quitting; Wally. I couldn't look him in the eye. He was laughing so hard he could barely say, "I told ya."

I had tried with all my heart and soul to quit. I was so determined, so close. As I put my helmet on that afternoon, I remember wondering *what happened? How was it I was still playing? Why?* For the last time, I wanted to quit. And very soon, I would realize why Andy wouldn't let me.

Chapter Seven

The Value of X and "Why"

---Langdon---
December 21, 2006 in Staunton, VA

I roll the plastic top of my water bottle between my fingers to occupy my time. I'm saying Bryan's lines right along with him as I've heard it so often in the past three months. It never gets old, and he delivers it better each night. My eyes scan the audience for familiar faces; my wife, some friends I play basketball with on Sunday nights, the teller at my bank, the guy who owns the coffee shop downtown who knows my regular order. I think how I know and appreciate all these different people and what they mean to me. That I had no idea when I was a senior in a cap and gown on this stage years ago, these very people I'm recognizing tonight are a part of my life.

Then my eyes connect with my high school Algebra-Trig teacher. I had no idea he was here tonight! In a classroom just upstairs in this very building is where I tried to prove to him that I would never need to know how to find the slope of X.

One early Monday morning, my sophomore year, my head was swimming with values of X and Y, variables, formulas, and a bunch of other trigonometry rules I didn't care

about. It was my turn to go to the board and
show that I understood my homework. There's no
way I could have understood it, because I didn't
do it. And there's no way I could have done it
since I didn't understand it. So with the chalk in
my hand, I boldly wrote on the board, "X=I
DON'T KNOW" and "Y=I DON'T CARE." The
entire class got a laugh from this. Well, okay,
maybe not the entire class. Mr. Higgs didn't
think it was all that funny. Clever maybe but not
funny.

Since it was now obvious I had no idea
how to work the problem to find the values of X
and Y, Mr. Higgs slowly sauntered up to the
board, took the chalk from my hand and began to
speak. "Langdon's answer is right. By itself,
nobody knows the value of X. It pretty much
means nothing. And by itself, nobody cares about
the value of Y. It means nothing, also. But what
I'm interested in is where these two meet. X is
walking down the road one day, wallowing in his
own misery and Y is on the other side of the road
minding his own business and then *Bam!* They
run in to each other. This is what I want to
know. This is what I care about. Where do these
two meet? By themselves, they are boring and
uninteresting. But once their paths cross, it's
gets good. They impact one another. They affect
each other. They feed off of each other. So don't
quit drawing Line X because it's boring. Don't
quit drawing Line Y because you don't care. You
never know where either one might lead and
whose line they'll intersect with. You can't quit."

Sitting there, still rolling the cap in my fingers, I chuckle with a realization of what he was talking about that day. He not only knew a lot more about math than me, he knew a lot more about life. His line had crossed with many others and those were the times he remembers and cherishes. And at that moment, I was cherishing the time his line crossed with mine. Thanks Mr. Higgs for not letting me quit drawing my line.

So if Bryan, the lineman, was X, then if he'd quit, he would have never have met his "why?"

Chapter Eight

Kennedy vs. Kennedy

···Bryan···

"Kennedy vs. Kennedy." This was the headline in the Nashville paper October my sophomore year. I remember this headline for a few reasons. First, somehow I was being written about in the paper. Second, I wondered *why are they writing about me?* I was just a skinny, lanky fifteen year old playing offensive and defensive tackle; I was only a lineman. Newspapers don't write about offensive and defensive linemen. They write about running backs and quarterbacks.

And speaking of running backs, there was one for the opposing team that week that was breaking all kinds of records carrying the ball. I had certainly heard of him and all of his accolades, but I got to know his number really well from watching him on film the week of the game. He would run, dodge, juke and jolt like most I hadn't seen. A lot of jealousy flared inside of me for just a bit watching him, thinking I could be doing this, too. But my thoughts never wandered too far, because Coach Flatt's voice would interrupt my daydreaming. Coach Flatt had all of us convinced that playing this Kennedy would require more than our best effort. There was no doubt to any of us sitting in that room watching this guy score touchdown after touchdown, that this player had an extra dip of "special" when it came to running the football.

And third, when I saw this headline I was very confused. Confused as to why I would be mentioned along side his name. I was not comfortable with this. After all, it wasn't Kennedy vs. Kennedy, it was their school vs. our school, their team vs. our team. I was not playing this guy alone.

The game came and went. Our team put forth another great effort, and we walked away victorious. I don't remember much about that night. I only remember that we won and it was terrible weather; cold, rainy, and lots of mud. And I remember as I walked off the field to the locker room, my position coach, Mickey Jacobs, put his arm around my shoulder pads and said, "You just got paid the highest compliment a defensive tackle could ever get paid."

I cut my eyes at him wondering who said what about me. It was a pretty uneventful night on my side of the field, and that was his point.

"They only ran to your side one time the entire game and you still made tackles all over the field!" He was so excited for me. It hit me then. Not the compliment but I realized why I was feeling down. They didn't run the ball to my side all night! How could this be good? This was boring to me. Certainly not fun. I hated being a lineman and now I guessed I hated being good at it. Coach Jacobs was another one of those "miracle" coaches, and I trusted his compliment as much as I trusted his coaching. But how could this be good?

Yes, we won, and I guess I should have been all smiles. Not me, I was still a lineman. And the mere joy of anything was instantly gone when someone reminded me of the fact that I was an offensive and defensive tackle. I wanted to be the other Kennedy in the headlines.

I showered and got on the bus to go back to my high school where I got on another bus full of a few teammates but more of other students. It was on this bus ride that I began to question everything. Everything. *Why? Why was I here? Why was I miserable? Why was I a lineman? And why were people talking about me? Why was my name in the paper? Why was it a compliment that they didn't run in my direction for an entire game but only once? And why am I still playing football?*

I stared at the rain on the window blocking out the laughter and excitement from the other students on the bus. They were happy to be on this bus and where it was taking them. It was dark, cold, and I was lost in a blank stare as raindrops raced across the window. It was as if I were staring at the three words that described my adolescent life at that time: dark, cold and lost.

Brentwood Academy, my high school, is a school that was founded on the "Triangle" philosophy. The three sides of the triangle are Spiritual, Academic, and Athletic. Honestly, when I was accepted into this school, I only cared for one side of this triangle, and it certainly wasn't academic or spiritual. As I sat there on that bus that dreary night, I was fully convinced I didn't care for any side, not even the athletic anymore. Yet, I found myself on a bus heading straight for the side I had perhaps least cared about: spiritual.

More questions shot through mind. *How did I get on this bus? Why did I sign up for a weekend spiritual retreat?* I reminded myself of the truth, the twisted intent of why I decided to go. I had seen on the sign-up sheet where there were going to be some cute girls on this retreat. All I had to do was sit through some talks about the Bible, and the rest of the time I could flirt with these girls. Sounded like a trade-off I could handle.

Friday night was getting to know some of the other students there and learning what to expect on one of these retreats. Saturday proved to be sort of boring. However, the food was good and there was plenty of free time. Saturday night there was to be a long meeting, and I was dreading it. This meant I had to sit and listen or at least act like I was listening. Nothing is worse than sitting and listening to people talking about things you don't really care anything about.

I made a point to sit in the back. I did my very best to act like I was paying attention, as I had plenty of practice at this five days a week in school. It was safe to say that I didn't want to be there. I just wanted the meeting to be over and just go run or get out and do something. I was alone. Alone in my thoughts, alone in this meeting, alone in this world. Or, so I thought.

Somehow some of what the speaker was saying began to grab my attention. Well, maybe not so much what he was saying but the fact that the girls sitting near me seemed to really be

paying attention. So I listened a bit more
intently.

Now let me stop and say right here that I
knew *of* God and I knew *of* Jesus. My
grandmother made sure of this. She made sure to
ask me if I prayed, and she made sure to remind
me to be a good Christian boy. So, like a typical
teenager, I pretty much thought I knew all of
this stuff already. I was hoping to get all of this
God and Jesus stuff over with.

But something happened that October
night that changed my life. I began to listen,
really listen. I began to hear about this Jesus
and how He came for us, came for me. Not only
came for me but even died for me. Really? For
me? Me? The miserable lineman? The one getting
praised for things I hated doing? The one with no
neighbors? The one that is a terrible student, the
one that knew he was stupid when he took tests?
The one that looked so good on the outside, yet
the one with all sorts of problems that no one
seemed to know about on the inside? The one
that wanted to quit it all? Me?

I looked around and saw people crying.
My friends crying. I felt like crying, I had felt like
crying for years perhaps, but, I was a football
player and we didn't cry. We had been
conditioned that crying was only acceptable
when you were in serious pain. A dislocated
shoulder or a blown-out knee. Crying meant
pain.

These eyes that had been looking through
a face mask my whole life now could see more
clearly even though they became moist and

quickly began to flood. *Wait! Wait! Am I crying? These are my tears! Stop! Stop crying!* I couldn't.

Physically, I knew what it was like to be injured, hurt, and in pain. I was used to the pounding, being blindsided, hospitals, trainers, doctors, and crutches. But this night I realized that I had been carrying a different kind of pain around for a long time. A different kind of hurt. So, I cried.

I am looking around at many others who were crying in this room yet they were also smiling. I had never seen that before. I did not know what this Jesus meant to my friends, I did not know exactly what Jesus meant or what this was all about. But I could see that He was real. I could see it in all the faces around me. Crying and smiling. Joy. Pure joy! That was it. They were experiencing joy! Joy because Jesus loved them no matter what. No matter how high or low their test scores were. No matter if they missed or made a tackle. No matter if you could recite Bible verses or not. No matter how short we fall of others' expectations. He loves you just because of everything you are; not everything you are *not*.

I wanted that. I wanted to know that. I needed that. As it turned out, so did my best friend, Wally. The only thing better than becoming a Christian, is having your best friend become one with you. He and I made a commitment that night, a commitment to ask Jesus Christ to come into our hearts. Wally and I became rookie Christians on the same night.

That October night changed me instantly. Not completely by any means, but instantly.

Kennedy vs. Kennedy. I will never forget that. The irony in that headline. Me against Me. My whole entire life had been Me against Me. A battle, a war. I needed a retreat. And thank God, literally, I got one.

Chapter Nine

Ride and Seek

---Langdon---
December 21, 2006 in Staunton, VA

As soon as Bryan finishes delivering this heartfelt *Steve's Bike* scene, Christmas music will seep softly out of the speakers while the lights will slowly rise to a dim, and intermission will begin. My off-stage duty is to make sure the correct CD is in the player with the music cued. He's about five minutes away from the end of his story, and as I have always done, I start to flip the CD over in my hand to make sure it's the right one. I catch a glimpse of myself in the reflection. The white fur trim around my Santa hat has lost some of its stitching and worn out like an old pair of favorite socks. The orange on my hat is so bright, even in the shadows of the side of the stage, it stings my eyes. And the correlation is that we all three, dressed in these outrageous and goofy costumes, are to represent, in a broader sense, the wise men in the Bible. How crazy is that? Three guys decked out like psychedelic Santas sitting around a campfire on Christmas Eve looking for answers to all the world's problems. Well, minus the Santa suits and the campfire, it happened about 2000 years ago, so why can't it happen everyday?

I recall performing the back half of the show in Canton, Georgia just a few weeks earlier, when I almost forgot to deliver my most powerful line. The left floodlight in the balcony blinded me for a moment and I got lost, for the first time, in the true meaning of what Wil's character, Big Daddy, was saying. He was thinking back on the wise men in the Bible and marveling at how far those men traveled and searched to find Jesus. He paused for a moment, stared out across the darkness of the audience and said, "Those wise men followed that star that night for thousands of miles. Thousands of miles on a horse or camel. Can you imagine doing that?"

I had heard him ask this question at least fifty times by now and always knew it as my character, Hamlet's cue to speak next. But that particular night, I got caught up in watching the show I was supposed to be acting in! I had practiced so hard to become Hamlet and just deliver the line with rehearsed feeling that I had overlooked what was really being asked. Hamlet was slow to deliver his line as Langdon, me, the actor playing Hamlet, was deep in thought, trying to imagine doing that. Would I get on a horse and travel thousands of miles to seek Jesus? Could I do it?

My follow up line is, "It seems like nobody thinks about Jesus the way those wise men did back then. You know, people today, including us, we let God seek us. We don't go seeking Him like we ought to." I told you it was my most powerful line. It makes a person think!

Bryan got on a school bus and traveled 40 minutes from his house to a weekend retreat and found Jesus. I travel across town every Sunday to seek Him. You may walk across the room to your bookshelf and pick up the Bible to find Him. All of our journeys are different, but none of them are far because He is everywhere. He's always waiting to be found. Some of us have always known Him, some of us have found Him later on. And some of you may be seeking Him right now. Good for you and God bless you.

Different times and stages in our lives prove to be more sensitive to His knowing. Sometimes the "Christian door" gets cracked open a bit and other times it's flung wide open. It was Bryan's time to find this new Friend and Strength in his life. He didn't know at first he was looking, but all the more, he found Him. Just as we are told: *But from there you will seek the Lord your God, and you will find Him if you seek Him with all your heart and with all your soul.* (Deuteronomy 4:29)

Chapter Ten

Philippians 4:13

---Bryan---

I can do all things through Christ who strengthens me (Philippians 4:13). This made sense to me. A fifteen year-old rookie when it came to God. From the moment I read this verse, I grabbed onto it tightly. I took it and applied it to all the things in my life that didn't make sense to me. I applied it to all the things in my life that I didn't particularly like, and the word 'hate' would be a word I would try not to use any longer.

I would need that verse almost immediately, too. We made the playoffs after the retreat that year, and the playoff game before the state championship we were matched against a great football team in Memphis. This game would see to it that I would spend a few more months with a new set of crutches. We won the game, but in the second half my left knee didn't have a chance to tell the 250lb offensive guard that it didn't bend *that* way. The all too familiar pops and instant pain raced to my ears and brain. I was out again. But if one can take something in stride on a pair of crutches, Philippians 4:13 strengthened my walk in more ways than one.

I recovered with a new intensity, a new
reason, and more than anything, I had accepted
whatever life brought my way. I was green when
it came to this new life, this new me, but I was
trying my best to go day by day. And with this
new friend, Jesus, on my side now, I felt stronger
than ever before to face those things that I would
have shied away from before.

As for football, I had no clue what was
happening. I remember the first letter I received
from a major college wanting me to come play
football. How exciting it was to see the team logo
on the envelope! I was in the tenth grade. It was
after the state championship game that year.
The letter asked me to fill out some information.
I think I might have skipped through all the
normal height, weight, bench press stuff. When it
came to the Comments section, I wrote
something like this: *Thank you for your letter,
but I am not interested in playing college
football.*

I had no aspirations of letting this football
thing go too far. I would be a lineman if God
wanted me to while in high school but that would
be plenty enough for me.

Day by day I went. That sophomore year I
was selected to the All Mid-State football team as
a defensive tackle. So here I was, this new born
in a new world, and I was not treading water like
before, I was swimming! My junior year proved
to be overwhelming in many positive ways, also.
I was getting piles of recruiting letters and visits
by all the major colleges. The logos on the
envelopes ranged from as far west as USC to as
far north as West Point Academy to as far south

as the University of Miami, and all in between.
Each day a new logo on an envelope would be in
my locker at school and more in the mailbox at
home. Literally hundreds. On one hand, it felt
great to be noticed, appreciated and wanted. On
the other hand though, I was not comfortable at
all with being singled out. It didn't seem right to
me. Football is a team sport.

Late in the fall my junior year, Coach
Jacobs would inform me of another
"compliment." "You made All-State defensive
tackle! As a junior, you made All-State!" He
explained to me that it was very unusual for a
junior to receive the honor. I was, of course, very
honored, but still somehow uncomfortable.

This being a Christian seemed to bring a
wonderful balance to my life in the past year and
a half. My grades had improved, my outlook had
certainly improved, and obviously the success on
the football field was prominent. I couldn't
believe the turn my life was taking. And it was
about to get better. Before practice began my
senior year, I had received perhaps the greatest
football gift since the sixth grade. Coach Flatt
had decided to play me at Tight End. Complete
joy filled my soul to the core when I heard this
from him. This meant that I would be catching
and running the football again! Wow! God really
knew what He was doing, didn't He! Finally!
Wally, John, and I were selected as team
captains, and this year was going to be the best
year ever.

Another factor added to the excitement
was Coach Flatt had kept this position change a
secret. He kept if from the press, the recruiters,

and most importantly, our first opponent that
year, Mt. Juliet.

It was fun keeping this secret from
everyone. Especially when it came time for our
first scrimmage that summer. (The first time we
would take the field in full uniform under the
lights in front of a crowd.) My entire high school
career I wore number 78. According to the rules
of football, a Tight End, or a person catching the
football, cannot wear a number in the seventies.
Therefore, I would have to change my number.
Coach Flatt didn't want anyone to know our
secret, so in that first scrimmage, he played me
at offensive and defensive tackle only, just like
my three previous years. I didn't mind being
number 78, because I knew it was only for the
pre-season. In fact it was kind of fun. Yes, I said
fun. I was having fun again playing football! My
life had found a new direction and a brand new
meaning.

Before the scrimmage, we spent our
football camp down in Georgia at an army
barrack, Camp Catoosa. Catoosa came and went
and soon enough it was show time! It was the
first week of the regular season. I was somewhat
surprised that week to see my picture in the
newspaper on the cover of the high school
football preview for the state of Tennessee. By
this point in the summer, I had talked with
Coach Flatt, asking him to keep all of the scouts
away from me. I was not comfortable with this
attention and frankly, I thought I was still
unworthy. He readily agreed to this request. And
the first game was coming up. Friday night.
Against Mt. Juliet.

I could not have been more excited. I couldn't wait. This was what all my years before had lead me to. This senior season. Team Captain, with my two best buddies, the grandstand full of scouts from all over the country, and most importantly, that night I took the field wearing number 86. I was officially a Tight End! I had an extra spring in my step as we warmed up. John throwing me passes on our end of the field. Glancing over at the other end of the field. Checking out the Mt. Juliet team. They were big, much bigger than us. And they had Butch Hamby. He was their quarterback, and he was good. They also had a linebacker with the nickname "Wolf Man." I was wishing I had a nickname. I looked down there from time to time hoping to catch a glance of either player but instead, I caught a glimpse of Coach Flatt standing next to the Mt. Juliet coach.

I didn't learn until thirty years later what was being said in the conversation that night. It pertained to the big surprise Coach Flatt and I had unveiled to the scouts and that opposing coach. Me playing Tight End. After their coach saw me during the pre-game warm ups wearing number 86 and catching passes, he said, "You better not be playing Kennedy at Tight End, Carlton. You better not line him up at Tight End!"

To say the least, he was shocked, unprepared, and maybe a little sore at being blindsided. Then jokingly he said, "Carlton, if you line him up at Tight End tonight, we're going after his knee."

Coaches love to joke around when they are nervous and both coaches were nervous. And not only were they nervous, they were cousins.

It was a perfect summer night for high school football! The stands were filled on both sides of the field at the home of the Mt. Juliet Bears. It was hot and humid and there was a suffocating haze of intensity settling over the field. It was thick and heavy, and I welcomed every ounce of it.

John was a great quarterback, and I would make sure to be his equal catching the ball. You never knew when or even *how* John would throw it to you. John Patton was the first guy I ever saw throw a pass behind his back! I remember thinking *I don't care how you get it to me, just get it to me. Throw it to me front-wards, backwards, sideways; just throw me the ball, just throw me the ball!*

Since that retreat my sophomore year, it was easy to see how God had brought me to a place of true bliss. I was doing exactly what I wanted to do, and I was exactly where I wanted to be. Everything in my life was on an upturn and for the first time, I sincerely felt happy.

The game was underway. The first pass was butter. The ball just melted in my hands. It was like an old friend that I had not seen in years finding me in a crowd of thousands of people walking around downtown New York City. My eyes focused on its departure, the white stripes like ribbons streaming through the air spinning like a ballerina, right towards my hands. John threw perfect spirals and he delivered this one perfectly to me. That leather

met my hands and I wish I could have frozen
that feeling forever. I would take that feeling out
right now and dance with it. I once again had the
ball in my hands, and I was running with it. I got
tackled and I hopped up, running back to the
huddle, again with a renewed love for this game.
All was wonderful, and all was perfect. I was
catching passes, and we were marching down the
field. Just a few drives later, John and I
connected for our first touchdown just before the
half. This was the kind of night that people
would talk about forever. A night I knew I would
never forget.

On the defensive side of the ball, I was
chasing Butch Hamby around the field, doing my
best to stop their offense so I could get back to
playing on my offense again. I don't know who I
hit, but I hit someone so hard it cracked my
helmet. This was something I didn't even realize
until halftime. We were all gathered on a knee in
the end zone. A few of the coaches were trying to
find another helmet to fit me. To this day, I don't
know whose helmet I wore that night, but I am
grateful for their head being the same size as
mine. I just wanted to get back out there. I
wanted the second half to start. This was so
much fun!

I got my wish soon enough. We had the
ball, and we were in the offensive huddle around
mid-field. John called the play. "Right 27 to the
tailback. On blue. On blue. Ready. Break." The
entire offense clapped simultaneously with all
eleven voices saying the word, "break" at the
same time. We each peeled away from the huddle
running to the ball, to the line of scrimmage,

taking our places and ready to get in our stances. I found my spot on the right side of the ball. I measured the distance between the inside tackle's right foot and my left foot, making sure that the gap between us was just right. I leaned forward in my stance and studied the players position in front of me. When the ball was snapped, John would hand the ball off to Wally who would be running right in between this gap between our offensive right tackle and me. All I had to do was kick the end out, and off Wally would go.

John began his cadence, "Down, Set, Red, Red." The line, including me, were waiting to hear the color blue, because we knew whatever he said after the color blue, we would fire off. There was a slight pause, and then John continued, only this time with a different color. "White." Again and louder, as if he were saying it in my direction for only me to hear. No, I couldn't see him, but I certainly heard him yelling. "White!" My ears perked up inside this borrowed helmet. "White" was code. An audible. John got behind the center and saw the huge gap on the right side of the ball just behind the defensive end. "White" was the code word for the tight end, for me. Code for a hot pass. When the ball was snapped, the original play was no longer what we were to run. This play was now going to be a pass and a pass to me. I was to take three steps outside the defensive end lined opposite me and turn around to the inside where I would find the ball being thrown to me very quickly. I loved to hear John change the play to "White."

"Blue. Hut!" Off I went out of my stance, there was no time to think, just react. I took my three steps outside and turned my head back inside to my left to find the ball that I knew would already be in the air. It was coming towards me, but not coming towards me in front of me, but rather high and a bit behind me. No problem. I stayed focused. I had caught others tougher than this. Still looking to my left, I had to turn both shoulders completely back towards John. I now had my back to the opposing free safety, which by now recognized this "hot pass" route. He was breaking on the ball, running towards me like a locomotive. I jumped as high as I could and I still needed to reach high into the air with both hands, stretching my body for every inch. The ball fell perfectly in my hands. My body still turning in the air, I came very close to completing a full 360-degree turn. But my body surrendered itself to gravity and found its way to the ground greeted first by my left cleat. As my left foot found the turf, all my weight landed on top of it. And before I could get my right leg down, well, I never did get my right leg down.

That Free Safety had found his target and running full speed, he torpedoed his body, helmet first, on my left knee. Bullseye.

If you have ever been in a traumatic car accident, or some sort of crash, or collision, perhaps you are more familiar than most with what I am about to attempt to explain. I was being catapulted in the air by the tremendous hit I had just received below. And while in mid-air, my world transformed into slow motion. My thoughts seemed to last an eternity before my body crashed to the ground. My first thought was, *this is really bad*. Then more thoughts slowly came and went. *This is going to be a long time getting ready before I can play again. I wonder if this time they are going to operate? I bet Dr. Lipscomb is going to yell at me for not letting him operate last time. How long will it be before I can play again, before I can catch the ball again?*

The ball. Where was the ball? I felt it still tucked to my side. I wish I would have thought of Philippians 4:13, but I did not. And if I would have, I am not sure I would have believed it.

The pain found its way from my left knee to my brain. I cannot and will not even try to describe the pain. At first, I felt it all and then I felt nothing, still in the air. Then I heard a flop! I hit like a rag doll. I lay there in the dirt motionless. Like a sack of feed dropped out of a hayloft landing with a big thump. The silence was deafening. I couldn't tell if I was breathing or not. It was so quiet. Butch Hamby, the Free Safety that hit me, was unconscious from delivering this bolt of thunder. It was the quiet after a train wreck. After all the screeching and entangling metal, everyone in the stadium was just silent, trying to assess what happened and the damage.

My eyes then popped open. I had them clinched so tightly I wasn't sure if they would even work when I did manage to open them. It took me a moment to focus. What I saw had to be some sort of illusion, but through the thickest of tears, I saw a cowboy hat resting on the field. A straw cowboy hat. I tried to focus on something else. I couldn't reason why I would open my eyes and find them looking at this cowboy hat. But the pain was too great, too immense to reason anything.

Unable to move, staring at this hat, I felt someone at my side. Someone kneeling next to me. I looked over to see the number 77. Andy. I knew that I needed to get up and get at least to the sidelines, but the pain wouldn't let me. All I felt that I could do was lie there on the field and cringe in my own pain, but Andy wouldn't let me.

Chapter Eleven

Number 77

···Langdon···
December 21, 2006 in Staunton, VA

Everyone is motionless and fixed on Bryan, who is approaching his last few lines of this scene about a kid named Steve and the bike he got for Christmas.

For fear of inadvertently attracting some kind of attention, I tip-toe back to that uncomfortable chair. It's as uncomfortable as those metal bleachers at every high school football stadium. And I imagine myself sitting there that night, that night that Bryan was blindsided and flipped around and about like an unlucky matador who just made a nostril-flaring bull really mad. I imagine myself wondering those same thoughts you might be wondering right now. *Is Bryan knocked out? How bad is the damage to his knee? Who is number 77? And why is there a cowboy hat lying on the field?*

If this audience only knew the real story Bryan was telling. This story is not about a kid named Steve, it's about a kid named Andy. Andy Anderson.

Andy was this number 77 kneeling down beside Bryan that night on the field. He was not

wearing a full uniform. He had on khakis. He
was wearing a jersey but no pads or helmet. His
name was in the program and he was listed as a
Guard. But he never played a down. He was on
the sidelines, always following the ball and
always within arms-length of Coach Flatt. He
loved standing by Coach Flatt. He would holler
at his teammates; nothing ever scolding, only
encouragement. His team support was obvious.
His love for the game was as if he were the most
talented, the most gifted, as if he were being
recruited by the world and would soon sign a
major college scholarship. And just like we know
Superman by his cape, everyone knew Andy by
his straw cowboy hat. Andy and Bryan went to
high school in a town not far from farm country.
Pick-up trucks, boots and cowboy hats weren't
that uncommon to see part of a young man's
attire. He wore it at home, wore it at the mall,
wore it in class and wore it at football games. But
Andy was no farmer or rancher; this hat didn't
signify his lifestyle, it served a different purpose.

    A few weeks earlier, Bob and Jo
Anderson, Andy's parents, had noticed Andy
having some serious and painful headaches. He
had a few seizures in the months before. Bob had
seen to it that Andy see the doctor about them,
and more importantly, the doctor see Andy. The
doctor just assumed it was a growing 16 year-old
boy experiencing some sort of growth change.
Still, Bob and Jo were concerned about these
symptoms.

    One day, Bob came home from being out
of town due to work. Andy had been in bed for a
few days sick, with presumably the flu. But for

some reason, he wasn't getting any better. Bob
took one look at the type of medicine and the
powerful dosage. Andy was not getting any
better. He went into Andy's room and after
talking with him, Andy told him about some
numbness he had in his hands. Something told
Bob that he needed to take his son to the doctor.
He could feel that something wasn't right.

        This was a very difficult time for Andy to
go see the doctor. Not just because nobody likes
to go to the doctor, but his bags were packed for
Camp Catoosa. The same Camp Catoosa Bryan
wrote about earlier. It was time to take off to
Catoosa County, Georgia, which is nestled in the
mountains just inside Tennessee's southern
border. This was the second week of summer
two-a-day practices and the entire team would
ride together on the bus. It was an attempt to
bond the team together.
        Although Andy had already been taken off
the roster to physically play football that
summer due to his headaches and seizures, still
he wanted to be there on that bus heading to
Georgia, because that's where his teammates
were going. And because that's where football
was. He loved football.

        On a usual Friday afternoon, Bob and
Andy pulled up at the doctor's office. It was a few
minutes before the end of the work day and Dr.
Fields had his golf bag over his shoulder headed

for the course. Bob explained to the doctor the
reason for the visit. And once he heard the
concern in Mr. Anderson's voice and saw the
unexplainable urgency on his face, as only a
worried parent can portray. He grabbed his
clipboard and asked Andy to come on back.
Questions were asked, x-rays were taken and
more wrinkles began to ripple across the doctor's
forehead. Once he heard about the numbness in
Andy's hands, Dr. Fields immediately made a
call to Vanderbilt Hospital.

If I may jump time here, I only do so to
tell you this. During our visit with Mr. and Mrs.
Anderson on a cold December Sunday afternoon
in 2008, Bryan and I sat at their kitchen table
while Mr. Anderson recalled this trip to see Dr.
Fields that Friday afternoon. This was the first
time during this visit that his voice cracked, his
lips quivered and a subtle tear fell from his face.
For me, it was the first time the realism of this
story was revealed. To see a father recall a
memory of his son, while watching his tears melt
into a smile, showed both the strength and the
struggle he and his dear wife have endured. The
tears were for the pain he felt for Andy. The
smile was because he was talking about someone
he dearly loved. His son. The son he tucked in
bed at night when he was little. The son he made
do his homework. The son he lit birthday candles
for every year. And the son he threw football
with in the back yard. I saw a father put his
head in his hands because he felt helpless that
he couldn't take on the pain and the seizures and

the headaches for him. I saw a man that
afternoon who proved to me that time can never
drown memories. And memories never fade
because of love.

     The Brentwood Academy Eagles were
spread out across the practice fields at Camp
Catoosa. The linemen over by the edge of the
woods, the backs closer to the barracks with
Coach Flatt. Over on two other practice fields
were two other teams attending the same week
of camp. Whistles could be heard in short spurts
from every corner of this camp. Commands were
barked out; some encouraging, some not so much.
A smile was nowhere to be found on a player or
coach on these fields. This was intense training
and practicing. The air was full of young men
proving themselves. The crunching of helmets
and pads colliding and bodies piled on top of one
another. Football was not intended to be played
in the thick August heat and these sweaty faces
and winded lungs were proof of it.
     A car pulled down the road to the practice
field and stopped at the far end zone. Out jumped
Andy, eager and ready as ever to be with his
teammates. Wally Knox and John Patton were
standing beside Coach Flatt with the other backs
when Andy came running across the field. His
face lit up with the first smile this practice field
had seen all day. With each step, Andy was
closer to where he wanted to be: on a football
field with his teammates. By the size of his
smile, Wally, John and Coach Flatt immediately

felt that this was a sure indication that all tests had returned negative.

They all knew where Andy had been and why he wasn't there with them. They knew about the headaches, the seizures. They were waiting to hear what the doctor said.

Coach Flatt stopped practice for a moment and greeted him. "What did the doctor say?"

With that same smile he had run across the field with, Andy responded, "I got a brain tumor Coach. I gotta have brain surgery."

Chapter Twelve

Bryan's Song

···Bryan···

We won the game that night against Mt. Juliet. I don't remember the score. It's funny how players don't remember scores but do remember wins and losses. I don't even know how I made it to the bus. But with ice packed on my knee, I rode the bus home knowing my world had changed, knowing that this injury was worse than any of the other ones I had experienced. I knew that it would be a long time before I would even be able to walk again, much less run or hit. I crawled into bed that night with pillows under my knee to elevate it. Still wrapped in ice, my mom would freshen every forty-five minutes, it even hurt to sleep.

The next morning, I awoke to see Coach Flatt standing at the foot of my bed. He had his usual smirk and some sort of joke, but when he took the ice off my knee, any trace of a smile evaporated. He found that same stoic face that I had seen when I had told him I wanted to quit a couple of years earlier. Only this time it was much different. He wouldn't look me in the eyes. He seemed to be shocked or gathering what positive words he might find or what lie he was going to tell. He just stared at my knee. It was huge with swelling, and it felt as if it was detached from me somehow.

I lay in bed that weekend. There were plenty of people that came to the house that Saturday and Sunday. Most of the players were used to me getting my knees hurt and knowing I would come back from it pretty fast. But this time it was different. I couldn't even get up to go to the bathroom. I was frustrated, hurting and once again, felt very alone.

There were a few parents of other players that came by to check on me. I will never forget that. It meant so much to me. They'd come back to my room, look at my knee and tell me how bad the hit was. They would describe what it looked like and what went through their minds when they saw it. They all consistently kept talking about the hit. The looks on their faces and the way they shook their heads when they relived the stadium-deafening blow began to scare me.

More than one would say, "Maybe God is trying to tell you something Bryan." When each one would say this, I'd listen intently because I know now that when God speaks, we need to listen. *What was God trying to tell me?* Then they would say the word that I had not visited in a couple of years. They continued, "Maybe God is trying to tell you to quit."

Did I hear that? Yes, I think I did! Parents were telling me that maybe God was trying to tell me that I should quit! My brain raced back through my entire life! Quit? You have got to be kidding me. Quit? That is something I tried to do at least three times! Quit? Now? Now that God has brought me

through all He has brought me through? To get
to this point, lying in this bed and quit now?
Quitting was the most distant thing from my
mind. I was a rookie Christian, but I knew in my
heart of hearts that God did not want me to quit.
Not now. Not after all we had been through! Not
a chance.

I knew I would recover. I knew I would
play again. I knew God had some sort of purpose
in all of this. I just had no idea that it had little
to do with playing football.

So I lay in my bed on my back and waited,
unable to sleep, unable to rest. I waited and
waited. The next few days came slow enough.
Doctor appointments, and of course, that nasty
word "surgery." I did not like that word. That
word could erase a smile quicker than any of
them.

I did make it back into bed that week
after seeing the orthopedic surgeon. I lay on my
back, with my knee elevated, and ice around the
clock for the rest of that week. It wasn't getting
better, it was getting worse, and I had developed
something they called phlebitis in my calf. I had
never heard of this, but I can tell you it hurt. My
whole leg felt like it could just explode it was so
swollen.

I lay there like a prisoner in my room. The
world was quite different for me now. No friends
coming over, no classes, no visitors, no
homework. I even started to wish to go back to
school. Just me in my room and occasionally,
Burford, our English bulldog would wander down
the hall to check on me. I was pretty much alone
with my thoughts, while outside the door to my

room the world kept turning. Pure loneliness had
moved in with me.

It was Friday night and we had a game in
Chattanooga. It was week two, and I had no clue
what was happening outside my door. I
remember the sun going down outside my
window that evening and thinking that the guys
were probably warming up on the field. I closed
my eyes and imagined the lights on the field. I
loved that feeling, that nervous energy warming
up before a game. I stared out the window for a
long while, missing all of them. I was missing my
teammates as they were some of the better
players and people I had played with. It was
their talents and hard work that got us to the
championships. I was missing the bus, the
fumes, and the idling diesel engines. Missing the
drums beating. That feeling I fell in love with
every night before each game.

The evening shadows began to fall against
my bedroom wall, and my attention turned to the
small T.V. Mom had brought into my room. My
mother took great care of me the best she could.
She wasn't big on me playing this game, but she
never said a word, not until my very last game in
college some five years later. It was then she told
me she was so glad I was done, and she no longer
had to worry. I never knew she did.

She'd bring my food and bags of ice
throughout the day. And she'd stand at the foot
of my bed, helpless, just watching me hurt.
Watching me frustrated and mad. Watching me
pick up a crutch and throw it at the door
puncturing a hole in the drywall. She could do
nothing to get rid of my pain.

The movie on T.V. was about football. I lay there watching it realizing it was about Gale Sayers, a great running back who had played for the Chicago Bears. I'd heard of this movie or, at least the book. *Brian's Song*. I watched for a long while and didn't realize the irony of its title and its subject until only thinking of writing this book. It's a story about Gale Sayers and his relationship he had with a teammate who had a terminal illness.

The phone rang and mom came back to tell me it was John Patton, our quarterback. I picked it up in my room, "Hello." I tried to sound like I was not crying.

"Sorry BK. We lost." That was all that was said and all I needed to hear. I placed the phone back onto the cradle and began to cry out loud. The kind of crying that you have to muffle with a pillow, the kind where you lose your breath. I don't know if I was crying because we lost, crying because I couldn't play, because I was hurting or because I was confused. I don't know. Maybe I was crying because of the story I had just seen on T.V. How it had affected me in some way that I wouldn't understand for years to come. *Brian's Song*.

Everyone has questions. Everyone searches for signs, for direction. Sometimes these signs are right in front of us. But sometimes it takes a lifetime or a life to see them.

Chapter Thirteen

The Bathtub

···Langdon···

We are met everyday with challenges.
Some are small. Like when I am running late for
a mid-morning program that my kids are
performing in at school and hit every red light in
town. It's not a big deal in the grand scheme of
things, but it sure is frustrating. God presents us
with these minor challenges, which more
accurately may just be annoyances, to see how
we will react. I *really* don't like to be late but at
the same time, I really don't like having my day
ruined because of a stoplight. It's not something I
planned on, but nonetheless, I can handle it. A
deep breath, a quick count to ten and a simple
prayer asking for an extra dose of patience, and
my kids will be happy to see that I made it.

Some other challenges are a bit more
serious. Like how Bryan's mother felt when he
threw his crutch against the wall because he was
angry, upset, disappointed, confused and
hurting. She knew all this. She wanted to snap
her fingers or click her heels to make his blown-
out knee all better.

And then there are others challenges in a
league of their own. Like Andy's parents
accepting the idea that their son has a brain
tumor, he is going blind, the right side of his

body is paralyzed and he is closer to drawing his last breath each day.

I don't know how a parent could ever get through this. It might seem to many that a temptation for a parent might be to give in and ultimately give up. I do know of what we are told in 1 Corinthians 10:13. *No temptation has overtaken you that is unusual for human beings. But God is faithful, and he will not allow you to be tempted beyond your strength. Instead, along with the temptation he will also provide a way out, so that you may be able to endure it.*

In other words, God won't give us more than we can handle. These words offer hope and assurance that we will get through whatever hard times and tribulations are presented in our lives. It reminds us that God is faithful in us, so in return, we must be faithful in Him that He will allow an "escape" from the pain. A way out of the struggle.

After visiting with Mr. and Mrs. Anderson for over three hours sitting at their kitchen table, there was still one thing I was curious about. So after we had hugged our goodbyes for the evening, I turned and asked Mrs. Anderson this final nagging question, "How did you get through it?"

She gripped the tissue she was holding in her hands a little tighter and with a teary smile said, "I had my bathtub."

The puzzled look on my face was obvious to her that I needed more. She continued, "Bob and I made it a point never to get upset in front of Andy. We knew he was dying and we were sure he did, too. But we tried never to show sadness or tears in front of him. But after he'd go to sleep, I'd go get in the tub and cry my eyes out. I needed this release. That bathtub was my escape from what I was dealing with everyday. Sometimes as early as lunchtime, if I felt my emotions welling up on me, I'd think to myself *Hang on Jo, if you can make it to the bathtub tonight, everything will be fine.* I feel like we all need our own bathtub in life."

Amen, Mrs. Anderson. Amen.

Chapter Fourteen

Ten More

---Bryan---

It was the fall of my senior year. Classes had only begun a few days before my injury. It was weeks before I could even bend my leg well enough to sit in a car, much less operate the gas pedal and brake. I spent the majority of the time being driven back and forth to the doctor's office to have my knee drained. Sometimes my mom would take me, other times John would take me and Wally would go along. It seemed each of us had injuries we needed treatment for.

A few weeks went by and after what seemed like enough ice to make an igloo and having the fluid drained from my knee several times a week, the combination of the two finally allowed me the mobility to get to school on crutches. And soon after, I gained enough flexibility in my knee to drive my truck myself.

Maneuvering through school and between classes was challenging. I learned how to walk with the crutches, but never learned to live with the pain of the phlebitis in my calf. The Velcro cast on my leg was good for keeping it straight but not a good reminder that I couldn't put any weight on my heel. Invariably, I would forget. I would naturally arrive at my desk and move the crutches to my side. A few minutes before the bell, I would try to stand. Let's just say this attempt left me more than once falling over chairs and desks forgetting the fact that I could not place any weight on my left leg. To say the least, it was painful. To say any more, it was embarrassing.

The entire school had a designated time each day called activity period. This was a time for everything from student body assemblies, pep rallies, to a time one could use for studying or playing basketball or just hanging out. It was a break during the school day. My activity periods were spent with only one activity. I was in the weight room sitting on an old Universal leg lift bench trying my best to rehab my knee doing leg extensions.

This was pretty much misery mixed with pain. I say this was our weight room, but someone today would never call it that. It was pitiful. There was a Universal Weight Machine, a leg extension, and a leg curl bench. This would be my home for the next ten weeks.

The room was more like a secluded dungeon underneath the basketball gym. There were only four white brick-o-block walls. No windows and that old locker room smell. No one ever went in there on purpose. Only when required.

The first day, I was lucky to do five total, with a two and a half pound plate added. And I wouldn't call it anywhere close to a "full" extension.

It was hard trying to be disciplined enough to spend my activity periods away from all the other students, and away from my

teammates, but activity period was not my only
time in the dungeon. I also had two study hall
periods each day, sixty minutes apiece. And, yes,
I spent those in the dungeon as well. Almost
three hours a day trying to lift my leg. Weeks
were passing by and I was not making much
progress. Then I began thinking that maybe
some of those parents were right. Maybe God had
given me a blatant sign, and maybe I just didn't
want to see it! Maybe I do need to quit! I didn't
know what to think. I was getting nowhere doing
the best I could. Or so I thought.

Isolated and alone for hours every day, I
sat on that machine. I tried to lift my leg over
and over. If any of you know what it's like to
rehab a serious injury, you know that finding the
will to do it by yourself takes a special breed. I
am *not* of that special breed.

I had made permanent palm imprints on
top of each side of the bench where I sat with
both hands gripping its sides. I squeezed that
bench so hard with my hands, feeling like I
would break it in two. I was staring at my knee
and wanting to cry. Not so much because it hurt,
but more so because it looked so horribly weak. I
would watch it quibble and shake as it tried to
lift the weights attached to the machine. I was
gritting my teeth when I saw this figure walk
into the weight room. This figure stood in the
doorway with a huge smile on its face and a
straw cowboy hat on its head.

"Hey Bryan, Coach Flatt told me I could
come down here and make sure you were
working out." He walked towards me and
stopped beside me as I was in the middle of one

of my monotonous repetitions. My leg almost extended to its destination. It was completely worn out.

Andy looked at me and then my knee. He had that big Andy Anderson grin on and said with a loud thunder, "Is that all you can do?" He was yelling at me! And he didn't stop there. He got louder. "Is that the best you can do?"

I was in shock. He was serious! My instant reaction was anger. I was thinking to myself *Wait a dang minute! I'm the football player here! Who are you to come in here and yell at me!* And all the while smiling. This angered me even more!

Who was this new friend of mine, or someone I thought was a new friend. Who was this guy standing beside me wearing a cowboy hat, a football letter jacket, a huge smile and yelling at me? I tried to reason what was taking place, why I had been verbally attacked. He stood there and waited for an answer. I didn't know what to say.

Quick, like when the ball is snapped and I react to the player in front of me, my instinct told me to treat Andy like I did on the practice field: give him a pass. So I said nothing. Then I began to think of his questions and I became even angrier. He wasn't giving *me* a pass!

Andy found a chair from the corner and he placed it facing me at the foot of this leg lift machine. He plopped himself down in this chair, never taking his eyes off of my knee. He began to talk as he stared at my knee. "How many have you done?"

For the first time I felt like it was time for me to talk, time for me to set Andy straight on a few things, so I started to explain to him what my usual routine was. He didn't let me get two words into my sentence. "How many have you done?"

He was yelling at me again! He was still staring at my knee, I was getting madder, and I couldn't even get him to look me in the eye. He wanted a number. He wanted to know how many I had done.

"Come on BK. Are you just going to sit there or are you going to start lifting?"

He kept barking orders and commands at me. Louder and more intense each time. I was beginning to wish that Coach Flatt hadn't sent him down here.

I was mad. In those fifteen or twenty seconds, I don't think I have ever been angrier. I wanted to tell Andy to stop yelling. I wanted to tell him to just shut-up! And if he would then I would explain to him that I was hurt! I wanted to yell back at him and say, "Come on Andy, I'm hurt! I'm doing the best I can here. And I don't need you coming down here telling me to try harder! Can't you see that? Can't you see that I am hurt? Didn't you see the hit? Didn't you see how bad it was? Didn't you see what happened to me? Can't you see I can't walk, I can't run, I can't, I can't, I can't!! I wanted to yell back and tell him he didn't understand.

But I didn't.

I saw for the first time who this guy in front of me was. I saw what gave him the right and what allowed him to yell at me, that allowed him to push me, to prod me, to provoke me, to make me mad. I saw what God had put in front of me.

My eyes focused past my knee and past myself. I began to see him. I began to see Andy. I began to see someone that had put aside all of his own pain, his own trials, his own uncertainty and tragedy. Someone who put his own life aside to help someone as selfish as me.

I was staring down at his cowboy hat. My mind recalled the few times I had seen underneath it. It was a straw colored hat but underneath it he always wore a light blue surgical cap.

I sat there staring at his hat as he was leaning over intently staring at my knee. It was as if he were lifting my leg for me, or trying to. He seemed to be straining as much or maybe even more than me. Instead of staring at my knee, I began to stare at this hat. Through this hat. I saw that 7 inch scar on the top of his scalp. As a seventeen year old boy, I had never seen anything like this before. The more I looked into that scar, the more strength I found in myself. That scar was proof that he had struggled and yet overcame.

Looking back on that day with those few moments, I can recall what I would describe as God's spirit move within me. I began to feel a peace come over me, a reasoning flow through me, and a gentle calmness I can't describe. One that came with much humility and embarrassment for my thoughts in those few previous moments.

I began to see someone, someone like I had never seen before, and someone that I knew who perhaps I could never be. This was someone that was suffering so much more than me and yet it was someone who volunteered to help me. To focus on me. To contribute to my life and taking it upon himself to push me. It was sort of understood between Andy and me that he knew he was never going to play again. By his coaching me and pushing me, this was his way of contributing to our team. He wanted me ready to play again for the playoffs. He succeeded. I have never been so humbled.

I began to lift. I shut my mouth and I shut my pride down and began to lift. I found in those next few minutes that I actually had a little more strength in my knee than the days and weeks before. I felt stronger that very instant. Stronger physically and stronger spiritually.

With the smoothest of transitions, his yelling turned into encouragement, that turned into motivation, that turned into incredible inspiration. He counted and yelled, and ended every tenth rep with, "Ten more! Give me ten more!"

And the only thing that saved me from his "ten more" was the bell for class. I would try to get up but he would push me back down on the bench. I was tired and wanted to quit but, Andy wouldn't let me.

Chapter Fifteen

Rear View Mirror

···Langdon···

Now it only takes a single college course of Intro to Religion to learn and fully realize that we are not on God's time. Our human minds can only conceptualize, process and understand that Time has a beginning and an end. In other words, Time is bounded by limits. God has Eternity. An infinite time. No beginning. No end. It just *is*. We use the word "eternity" to describe what God knows and uses. It's a word to attempt to explain what God's watch may look like. An attempt to relate to His reasoning. It cannot be understood; just accepted.

The best way to accept this, and sometimes the only way, is to realize the power of God's Providence. God's Providence is our roadmap. We don't know where we are going till we get there. And once we're there, we look back and don't know how we got there. There is no ride such as sweet as the journey.

The difficult part is when bad things happen to us. Things we feel we didn't cause, deserve, ask for or sign up for. When things are good, it's so easy to thank Him and give a spiritual high-five and stroll right along, cheering up our brothers along the way. But put a speed bump in our path, or even worse, a major obstacle, any fault lines in our faith begin to show. How much we allow these fault lines to crack is up to us. The biggest chisel to drive into them is Doubt. Not doubting ourselves, but doubting God. And the way we find Doubt is by needing to understand *why?*.

We are geared or wired, if you will, to accept reward without needing to know why. We call it a blessing and move on. We are grateful for it and may wonder about it, but we don't have that burning desire or struggle to *need* to know. This is okay and certainly natural because it's the way God made us.

Because God is so much bigger and smarter than we are, he also gave us each a rear view mirror. A mirror to look into, while still moving forward, we can look back to see exactly why we are on the path that we are traveling. Sometimes those roads we are traveling are paved. This is good. But sometimes those roads are dirt and we kick up a lot of dust so that when we look back, it's not clear as to what happened or why it happened. It takes some time for that dust to settle so that we may see again. But all the while, we're still moving forward on this road, this path.

I am a believer that God has His hands on the wheel of my life. Mine are on there, too, but if I start to turn down the wrong road, He tugs that wheel back on course. Most of the time I ask Him to. But sometimes He does it just because...well, just because that's what He does.

Bryan's life is about to take a hard left turn but in the right direction. He's about to go down a road he's never been on before. God's hands are still on the wheel and this journey is going to have another passenger sitting in the back seat. A passenger that knows the way. A passenger that Bryan didn't realize was riding with him until he looked into his own rear view mirror.

We are never sure how God will use a tragedy. We only hope that time and the goodness of others will reveal how a tragedy is used for a better purpose beyond our initial understanding.

Chapter Sixteen

That Red Truck

···Bryan···

We all have those certain birthdays that
we can't wait for and ones that we look back on
as being memorable and one of the better ones.
My sixteenth birthday was both of these; I
couldn't wait for it and thinking back on it, it
was one the best. The reason it was one of the
best was because at sixteen, I got my "freedom
card." That's right, my driver's license. Only I
would have to wait a bit longer than most
because I flunked my driver's license test. I was
so embarrassed. I remember Mom taking me
down to the Highway Patrol Station and sitting
in front of that machine, the whole time sweating
inside my brain. Now I was no stranger to a
white paper being marked up with red ink. All
those little round multiple choice circles looked
like the right answer to me! Looking back on my
test-taking skills, or more accurately, lack of, I
can see now why I ended up a songwriter. Even
at sixteen, I was seeing words like most did not. I
was arranging them and twisting them around in
my head. Well, this turned out to be what I'd do
for a living. I take common words and arrange
them and twist them around to form a verse or a
chorus to marry up with a melody. You know
sometimes our true gifts are revealed only when

we fail in other areas. So, to those of you who don't test well... there's hope!

My next attempt proved to be successful and though I didn't have a car of my own, having the driver's license was good enough. It wasn't until my senior year that my dad gave in to my wants and wishes, and bought me a red pickup truck! I could not have been more excited to know that my senior year I would be driving this beautiful red machine with the big moon buggy tires. I tried to hold the excitement in as much as possible, and needless to say, I couldn't wait to get it.

Now imagine yourself all psyched up and ready to see this truck sitting in the driveway when you get home from your first football game your senior season. Imagine the anticipation of jumping on that bench seat, cranking up that three fifty-four motor and hearing that rumble you had imagined forever! I was to receive the truck when I got home after the Mt. Juliet game. My dad said it would be in the driveway. And he made good on his promise.

He drove me home that night, his headlights flashed by that shiny red machine, and I just slumped deeper into his back seat. I wanted so bad to jump out, crank it up and drive away from all of this! It was a nightmare. Because all I could do was waddle on my latest set of crutches and look at it from the sidewalk.

It would be days before I could even get up and go outside, open the door and smell that new truck/car smell! I'd make it as far as the living room window and stand propped up on my

crutches and look at it in the driveway. When I
did finally make it outside, it somehow made it
worse. My leg would not bend, and I was too tall
to even get in the drivers seat. So I spent the
first three or four weeks just staring at that red
truck.

To this day, I don't think I thanked my
dad enough for this beautiful gift. I think I was
too lost in my own pity to even realize the
sacrifice he made to get me that truck. So, to my
dad, I am sorry I never did thank you enough,
and I am sorry that I was thinking only of me.
This seemed to be the natural pattern of thought
at this time in my life. Thinking only of me.

Weeks went by and I still couldn't bend
my leg enough to get in my truck. It just sat out
in the driveway, looking as lonely as I did,
begging for attention. So I called a good friend to
come over and put some speakers in the kick
panels. John Rippy was cutting wholes with a
jigsaw in the metal of my truck before I had ever
driven it. He got the speakers in and I put a new
tape deck in, and from that moment on I would
go outside to just spend time with my truck. I
would put a Merle Haggard tape in the deck,
then I'd go around to the rear of the truck to put
the tailgate down. I'd manage to crawl up in the
bed, rest my back against the cab facing the rear
of the truck. I'd just sit and listen, staring out
into the woods up at the stars. Just me, my
truck, and Merle.

I spent hours and hours in the bed of that
truck before I ever drove it. And not all of my
time back there was just sitting still. Most of my
time was spent riding in the bed of it, stretched

out while my little brother Shelby drove me to
school and dumped me out at the front door.
That's right. Me riding back in the bed, being
carted to school by my little brother. Now, that's
every senior's dream isn't it?

But, soon enough I was able to get enough
mobility in my leg to sit in the drivers seat and
work the pedals, at least enough to drive. I have
to admit to that being a pretty big motivation to
get my knee to bend!

That red truck saw it all. It saw every bit
of my life for the next five years. I guess it was a
part of me in many ways, and I think those that
knew me then couldn't imagine me without that
truck. I have never been prouder of any one thing
I was ever given.

As the saying goes "if that truck could
talk…" Well, I would have gotten into a lot of
trouble I am certain, and I might have stayed out
of a lot of trouble, and it for sure would have told
on me for driving too fast trying to get home for
curfew. I drove it hard and still it kept me safe
all those years. It knew my girlfriend, it knew
where I liked to eat, it knew my chocolate milk
cartons in the floor board, it knew Don Williams,
Hank Jr., The Statler Brothers, The Ohio
Players, Rick James, and Eddie Rabbitt. It knew
John and Wally all too well and some odors it
most likely didn't appreciate too much! It knew
its way to Oxford, Mississippi on its own. And we
were both lucky enough to know Andy Anderson.

Andy and I began our trek together
during all of our study halls and activity periods
in high school. And it was in that high school
weight room that Andy would be waiting on me

every time I would hobble or eventually limp in.
He was relentless on making me work, and he
did not care to hear that it hurt or it was killing
me.

Maybe you should go back and read that
last phrase again. I said "or it was killing me." A
phrase that pierces my heart as I write this. I
have a hard time dealing with my using that
phrase to describe something so trivial that had
happened to me.

You must realize by now that I had a knee
injury, and Andy had a brain tumor. I was being
helped, pushed, motivated, and inspired by
someone that was injured far more severe than
me. I was being served by someone that wasn't
facing missing a game or the playoffs, or at
worst, missing the season. I wasn't even being
helped by someone that could never play football
again. I was being served by someone that was
essentially fighting for his life.

Each day passed with Andy sitting in
front of me, intently focused on my knee, forcing
me to do ten more, and then pushing for another
ten more. I couldn't believe what I was seeing.
He never talked about his surgery. He never
talked about his tumor. He never talked about
his situation. Not once did he ever say anything
about himself and what he had been through, or
what he was going through. He just carried that
smile underneath that cowboy hat and focused
his strength on me. All on me. It brings tears to
my eyes to think of his unselfish behavior and
my lack of complete recognition for it at the time.

Andy and I spent a lot of time in that red
truck. In fact, we spent more time in that red

truck than any other person I knew. On a regular
basis, we were both scheduled to go downtown to
the hospital: mine to drain the fluid from my
knee and Andy's for chemotherapy. We were
supposed to check out of school in the office
before leaving campus, but Andy and I were
"regulars" for leaving campus. We'd meet by the
door and walk together to the truck. By this time
there was a hint of fall in the air. He would have
on his letter jacket and his cowboy hat. We'd hop
in, I'd crank her up, and off we'd go. Not saying a
word.

Andy would sit over across the bench seat
and cross his legs. He always wore that smile as
he'd sit quietly looking out the front window. I
think back on those days and can't help but to
wonder what might have been his thoughts. I'm
sad to think that I was probably not a good
friend to him because I didn't know what to say.
I didn't know how to act. I didn't know how to
talk to him about what he was facing. Was I
being a good friend by not bringing any of it up?
Or was I a bad friend for not bringing it up and
being someone he could talk to about it? I'll never
know.

I would swing my truck by Vanderbilt
hospital and Andy would hop out without saying
a word, shut the door behind him and kind of jog
towards the entrance. I remember having a
sinking feeling in my stomach as I watched him
jog to the door. I felt helpless. I didn't know what
to do. I wanted to do something, just *something*
to make it better. I'd slowly pull away and head
over to St. Thomas Hospital where my doctor
was and then swing back by to pick up Andy on

our way back to school. Day in and day out, this was our routine.

I have no idea how many players have suited up for Coach Carlton Flatt. I have no idea how many of those men were awarded scholarships to play Division I collegiate football. I have no idea how many of those men went on to play in the NFL. It's definitely a lot! These players are what most would consider to be obvious standouts in Coach Flatt's coaching history. He has, no doubt, had a profound impact on each player and I'm sure no player will ever forget him. But I do know of two boys he was around that *he* will never ever forget and neither one ever played a down in a game. The first being Chris Bonds, a classmate of my older brother who had muscular dystrophy. The other, Andy Anderson. Both were men among boys.

Coach Flatt's humility would never allow him to tell what I'm about to tell you. In fact, when Langdon and I interviewed him for this book, he never mentioned it. I only discovered this little known fact when talking to Andy's parents in December of 2008.

Mr. Anderson explained that on Andy's third night in the hospital following his surgery, that he was told by the nurses, his wife, and Andy himself, that he did not need to spend the night at the hospital. He left very late and returned at 5 a.m. the next morning in order to see the doctor when he made his early rounds. When he entered his son's room, Andy was all

smiles. The first words he blurted out, "Coach
Flatt came to see me last night!" Bob questioned
Andy as he thought he had been dreaming. Andy
emphatically let his dad know that indeed Coach
Flatt had held his hand and told him that he had
been thinking about him. Bob learned later that
Coach Flatt had indeed found his way to Andy's
room in the wee hours of the morning. He never
did figure out how Coach made his way up eight
floors in the middle of the night without getting
stopped by security or staff at the nurses'
stations. The winningest high school coach in the
state of Tennessee. A miracle coach.

Andy was in the hospital a week with his
surgery. He was at Brentwood Academy's first
football game a few days after being released
from the hospital. And it's of no coincidence that
this was the same game he ran on the field to
pick up that sack of feed that fell from the
hayloft, me. I was beginning to understand that I
was the X and he was my "why."

He went to every game that same season,
including all the away games, traveling with the
team on the bus. In the locker room after each
game, Coach Flatt presented Andy with the
game winning ball. These balls, with the names
of the teams, the date, and the scores, lined the
bookshelves in Andy's bedroom.

We went to the State Championship that
year but lost to a great team from Maryville,
Tennessee. Andy saw to it that I played in every
playoff game, and I owe him for that. Those

previous ten weeks of his relentless chants of
"ten more!" made me healthy and strong enough
to compete.

Along the way, I signed a football
scholarship to the University of Mississippi. Do
you remember the first recruiting letter I
received when I was a sophomore? The one in
which I replied that I did not intend to play
college football? Well, the coach who sent me that
letter was the very coach in the room with my
dad when I signed my scholarship. After I signed
at the bottom of the scholarship, Coach David
Lee (yes, the same David Lee that brought the
Wildcat offense to the NFL with the Miami
Dolphins) reminded me of that letter; in fact he
had kept it and showed it to me later. Looking
back, I can now see God's hand was on me and I
am so thankful His hand gave me Andy. All
those times I wanted to quit, God knew that if I
did, I would not have experienced His angel.

Football season ended, and the very next
day basketball season started. My workout and
therapy partner and I were sort of separated
while I was in basketball, but after Andy learned
that Wally and me were heading to Ole Miss, he
was quick to make his college choice. He signed
up to become a Rebel too.

I will be honest and say that when I heard
of his decision, I was saddened. I knew that Andy
had never even been to Oxford, Mississippi. I
knew that his only reason to choose this school
was due to the fact that Wally and I were going
to be playing ball there. And I knew what college

ball was like. It was a sixteen hour day job. I
knew that once that first horn sounded to wake
up at 6 a.m., my life was forever different. I knew
I would not get to see Andy much, if any at all.
And regretfully, I was right.

Andy and I still had the red truck rides.
There were holidays that I would return home,
and I'd get a call from Andy. The rides were no
different than the two of us going to the hospital.
He was just happy being in that truck and so was
I. And we made the four-hour trip to and fro
many times. The only difference was that with
each trip, I would see a different Andy. I began to
see a tired and a weaker body. And soon someone
that was carrying his arm a bit lower than
normal, someone that was having trouble
carrying his books and holding on to things.
Again, not sure exactly what to do, I think I tried
to ignore it. I tried to place it somewhere outside
of my reality. I didn't know how to deal with it.
Maybe Andy didn't either and maybe that's why
we didn't talk about it. I do know that I miss my
traveling buddy, I miss that smile, and those
bright eyes.

That red truck was our oasis. It was like a
get a way for both of us. And though he never
said much, I'm so glad he was there. He didn't
try to please me, he didn't try to impress me; he
was just Andy. And I loved him. You need to
know that without any effort, he changed my life
and so many others. Andy was my passenger,
and I was his passenger. We rode together. We
were partners. We were buddies. We were what
some today would call "soul mates," except we

really were. We were connected by our souls, our souls that belonged to Christ.

Wally and I got the message during football practice in the fall of our sophomore year at Ole Miss that Andy had passed away. We made that trip to Nashville and back to Mississippi that same day in that red truck. John Patton and I were asked to sing at his funeral. The road home was never the same, the red truck was never the same, and I was never the same. I am so blessed for all those times with Andy riding shotgun in that red truck and in my life.

Chapter Seventeen

Click, Click, Click

---Langdon---

    Click, click, click. I remember that sound. I was a senior in high school taking an English test on the first three chapters of the classic *Madame Bovary*. I was trying to recall what little of the first chapter I did read and trying to fake my way through the rest of the answers. In the row beside me was Clint. Let's just say that Clint was a pretty bold and wide-open character. I enjoyed his company for all the wrong reasons. And for whatever reason, Clint enjoyed mine. Every day after lunch, Clint would click his newly purchased class ring on the side of the wood veneer desk. The hollow cavity of this out-of-date school room desk would reverberate his heavy clicking so everyone could hear. Whenever Clint would start his "jewelry-thudding", I knew he wanted my attention. Whether it was the answer to question #3 or a frivolous comment about a classmate, Clint knew he had an audience in me and would beckon it with that click of his ring.

    Click, click, click. The unique sound of metal gently striking polished chrome. Another class ring, only this one not tapping the side of a desk, but the chrome side of a hospital bed. A ring with a tiny engraved football player with the

number seventy-seven on one side and the
Brentwood Academy triangle on the other. This
was the second Brentwood Academy high school
ring to wrap itself around Andy's ring finger. The
first one, Andy lost at Melrose Pool Hall not too
far down the road from Brentwood, Tennessee. It
seems he was hustling his dad in pool and
though he won the games of pool, he accidentally
lost the ring there. Andy loved that ring. He was
very proud to wear it and when he lost it, Bob
and Jo knew it had to be replaced, so they got
him another one.

Click, click, click. Andy was at home in
bed. Not his regular bed but a hospital bed
donated by the Anderson's church. It had been
moved to a small bedroom near the front door. A
door that remained unlocked day and night since
Andy had returned from Ole Miss in the early
fall of 1981. He had returned home for good. He
knew that a shorter life than usual was
imminent, and that a better day was coming
soon.

His health had deteriorated tremendously
the beginning of his sophomore year. He had lost
the use in his right arm, his body very weak, and
he had lost his eyesight. Because he had no sight,
he therefore had no sense of time. He didn't know
if it was 2:00 p.m. or 2:00 a.m. Jo, his mother,
recalls Andy tapping that ring one morning
around 2:00 in the morning. *Click, click, click.*
She shuffled through a dark quiet house into the
room where he lay to see what he needed.

"Mom, I want some fried eggs."

Jo, with a tired smile said, "Okay." She
then shuffled off to the kitchen and fried Andy

eggs. She later explained that he didn't eat very well and basically, "If he wanted fried eggs, then he was gonna get fried eggs. I didn't care if it was 2:00 in the morning!"

After this, another piece of furniture was added in that new makeshift bedroom: a lounge chair at the foot of Andy's bed. This lounge chair would be occupied every night during the last six weeks or more of Andy's life. Bob Anderson would sit, read, talk and sleep in that chair day and night. He would also take great care to record the amounts of fluids Andy was getting and how much he was losing. He kept immaculate records, the doctors claimed better than anyone they had ever seen.

Bob worked in sales and his income depended on the commission he made with clients. In order to establish clients and accounts, it meant a lot of traveling. On some of these trips, he'd take Andy with him. Father and son together in a car listening to music, sharing laughs, good times and quiet moments, all the while making memories that only Bob will cherish the rest of his life.

He compromised his work time and family time as best he could, but made the decision the last year Andy was alive, to stay home. He wanted to and needed to.

The phone call to his superior to let him know that he wasn't going to travel for a while was a nervous one. It was a tough company to work for as they focused heavily on the success of face-to-face meetings and the importance of being a hands-on salesman. Bob assured his company that he would keep in touch with all his clients by phone and be available to meet the satisfaction of these clients. He'd be sitting in that chair at the foot of Andy's bed. His superior was kind and understanding to allow this and would then determine if sales suffered. This was an especially risky time, as the company was already experiencing a drop in their sales because of market decline.

About a month went by and Bob received a call from his superior concerning his latest work schedule. "I just wanted to call and let you know that since you've made the decision to stay home with Andy, not only have your sales gone up, but the company's have gone up, too."

Bob confessed that logistically speaking, none of this made sense. And he also quickly confessed that when God intervenes, none of it has to make sense. His hand is on us all, and we are to accept what is given to us.

Few of us can imagine what this must have been like. I was trying to hold it together as I listened to these two incredible people talk about their late son, and how Andy never separated himself from his two brothers and sister. How he fit right in. How he never complained or said that he had it harder than someone else or they had it easy compared to him. That's when I heard Jo mention Andy's youngest brother, Matt. She said, "Of course about the time Andy got really bad, Matt was diagnosed with leukemia." I couldn't believe my ears. She went on to say that she pretty much took care of Matt, taking him to get his chemotherapy while Bob took care of Andy. I was beginning to see what made Andy the hero he was. This apple fell straight from the tree. I remembered meeting Matt back when we performed *MistleToe Roaster* at Brentwood Academy, so I knew he was a cancer survivor. I wanted to know more, so I sat and listened.

One of the last trips outside of this bed was one to their church's ball field. After the service on a Sunday morning, there was to be a dedication at this field. Andy found enough determination to sit in the chair in the den so his dad could get him dressed. Bob lifted him over his shoulder to try to complete the task but they both ran out of energy. With both of them out of breath, Bob looked at his son and told him not to worry with it, they didn't have to go. Andy nodded his head to say, "Yes, we do. I want to go." At this moment, Andy's youth director, John Gilbert, pulled in the drive and walked in the front door. The two men got him dressed and helped him to the car. Bob drove, with Andy riding shotgun and John in the back, on their way to the Forest Hills United Methodist Church.

They pulled up to the field just as the service was letting out. Andy rolled down his window and even though he couldn't see the pride on his churchmates' faces, he could hear every word that was being said. And then he heard over the loud speaker, "This field will be known as the Andy Anderson Field, as it is dedicated, to Andy Anderson."

A hospital bed and a lounge chair shoved into the small bedroom of the house close to the unlocked front door. And that unlocked door was a revolving door for Andy's family, friends, and a man that was very close to Andy. A man named John Gilbert.

As I mentioned earlier, John Gilbert was Andy's youth director. He came to see Andy frequently. The Andersons told us that John would come sometimes in the wee hours of the morning and they would not know that he had even been there. He would just walk in the front door, spend time with Andy, and quietly leave just as he came.

Now when I first think of all those that were going to see Andy, my first inclination is to feel sorry for him, and think of all those people that were faced with seeing him in this condition. If we all admit it, it is difficult at times to witness things like this. But after speaking to everyone Bryan and I interviewed, well, it seemed Andy was teaching everyone else something. They were not going to see Andy because they felt sorry for him, they were going to see Andy because he was helping them! Caring for them! Encouraging them.

Andy was home from Ole Miss after Christmas of his sophomore year. It had been almost three years since his first surgery. His health was so poor he would not return for the second semester that year. Instead, the decision was made to go back in for a second surgery. There was not much hope they could completely get rid of the tumor, but the goal was to at least try to get his vision back. He loved to read and loved to watch television. So the decision was made. However, the outcome was unsuccessful. He remained blind.

He never complained to anyone. Instead, he called on his youth director, John Gilbert. He asked John if he could have a Bible study with him. He let John know that it was his desire to increase his faith. Those were Andy's direct words, "I want to increase my faith."

Other than Andy's parents, it was John that spent the most amount of time with him during his last months. Bryan went to talk to John Gilbert. He came back from that meeting and shared these words from John with me:

Andy demonstrated tremendous faith, even in his blindness. What a blessing for me. I was like a big sponge. I was growing in my faith because of Andy's desire to grow in his. I was receiving so much more than I could give. Here I thought I was leading Andy in the Bible study, when he was really leading me.

Click, click, click. Bob and Jo admitted that they still to this day, out of nowhere, hear Andy's ring click on the side of that bedrail. Just another way of Andy letting them know that he is still with them.

Chapter Eighteen

Jogging My Memory

---Bryan---

It had been almost thirty years since that Mt. Juliet game. And it had been a little over twenty-five years since Andy passed away. I had written that story about *Steve's Bike* for the play in a chalet in the mountains of Gatlinburg, Tennessee. I was alone for a few days and had no idea that Andy would grant me his presence in that chalet, too. But there he was, front and center in my thoughts after all of those years. I did not fight the recollection of events or the replay of my time with him. Instead, I welcomed it. At least at first I did.

I guess you could say I allowed enough of my experience with Andy to resonate in my pen. It was hard to look at, hard to get on to paper. I was much too close to this fictional character Steve, much to close to my real old friend Andy.

Mistletoe Roaster was in production for the Christmas season of 2006. After its last show in Staunton, Virginia, I drove home in my truck thinking through the past few months of performing. I loved my time with Wil and Langdon. I loved all of our laughs and zany road stories. I loved the reaction of the audiences and the kind, heartfelt words they shared after seeing the show and receiving its message. As I passed through the Blue Ridge Mountains, I began to try to find another topic to think on. It seemed as when I'd continue to think of the play, my thoughts would always land back on *Steve's Bike*, and ultimately Andy. I will admit to some relief of knowing I wouldn't have to perform that scene again.

It wouldn't be too far down the road that I would pass the exit for Virginia Tech. It was then that my thoughts would turn from Andy to the campus shootings that had occurred there a short time before my passing by. I thought of all those innocent students, so young, just like Andy in many ways. My mind had found its way back to my old truck-riding partner again as I traveled farther down the road.

Once back home in Brentwood, Tennessee where I made my home, I let my world turn to other writing projects, both in music and to my first novel. I have always felt a great way to free my mind from anything I am currently working on, is to go outside and do something athletic. I love to mountain bike and I love to run. Either one of these activities will always take me to a place far from my current project. Well, at least they usually do.

Daily, I would head off to the YMCA where I would take advantage of the beautiful jogging paths meandering through Maryland Farms office park, and then continuing on past my high school, Brentwood Academy. This jogging time to me was a time to think on bigger things and to pray. My first mile would be spent mostly thinking of how my knee felt that day and pretty much talking myself out of any discomfort.

Then my mind would turn to nature. The trees,
the flowers, the sunshine and how I just enjoyed
soaking up the heat. I usually began my prayers
by thanking God. Thanking God for everything. I
would list my family and friends. No particular
order. I would just start with someone and end
with someone. I never planned on praying for
anyone in particular. I just let the names come as
God see fit to lay them on my heart.

From my dad, my mother, my brothers,
their families, to those who gave me my first
jobs, those who took time to teach me how to
write, and on and on. I would ask that God
forgive me for those I knew I hurt and for things
I was ashamed of. I would thank God for my
blessings, all the while jogging down this path.
And then out of no where, *wham!* Andy. There
would be his name in the forefront of my mind
every single time.

*Shouldn't this be something I have
already worked through?* I would think to myself.
Day after day, week after week, I had the same
experience. As soon as I would near Brentwood
Academy, my prayers would turn to thoughts,
and thoughts I was not prepared for. God really
knows how to get my attention!

As I jogged, one step in front of the other,
I let my thoughts go where God would take them.
They would usually go back to that night that I
lay there crying in my bed. That night I felt so
sorry for myself. A time when my whole world
had seemingly come to an end. Everything that I
had planned, everything that was going so
beautifully had changed. I went back to

remembering my tears. I thought of all the times
I wanted to quit. All the times I wanted out.

I'd think back on the friend that I didn't
know before he was diagnosed with a brain
tumor, the friend that was not as talented or
gifted in football as I was. The friend that would
have given anything to have had my ability for
the game, and if he had had it, he would have
certainly never tried to quit. The thoughts just
kept pouring over me.

Andy saw me hurt and came to my side.
He helped me off the field. He listened. He
encouraged. He supported. And he pushed me
through my rough times.

I would jog past the street where my dad
still lives to this day and the house that I was
confined to in my bedroom my senior year with
my busted knee. I remember so vividly that night
I sat in my bed crying. It reminds me that I
never once thought about my friend who lived
only three miles back down the road I had just
jogged. What must have been going through
Andy's mind? He was diagnosed with a terminal
illness. He wasn't facing a season ending injury.
He wasn't worried about how many games he
would miss. He was facing a fight for his life. I
felt so ashamed.

I jogged by that school a hundred times
over the next year or so. Each time thinking of
Andy. Seeming to attempt to know him better.
To do something to pinpoint the exact reasons for
these thoughts that continued flooding me. I felt
so many emotions. The main one being guilt.

How could I have been so selfish? I prayed that God would forgive me and that Andy would forgive me.

Maybe many of us have memories that we discover later in our years. I am thankful for God taking me through mine, though painful they might be at times. I realize that it is through this pain that we see God for what He really is. He is not only a great healer, but He is a God that shows us, who showed me through Andy all these years later, how to truly bear fruit. Good fruit. He showed me how to love. I am encouraged to know that God's fruit has no annual season. It can be harvested thirty years later. And it can produce a bountiful crop.

Andy would show me back then what true friendship is. He would show me what being unselfish truly is. He would show me Christ without ever preaching to me. He would show me what Paul describes in the Bible as 'the fruits of the spirit.' Paul lists them in Galatians 5:22-23; *But the fruit of the Spirit is love, joy, peace, patience, kindness, goodness, faithfulness, gentleness, self-control.*

How many people do we meet in our lives, in our *entire* lives that represent all of these? When we do meet these people it is as if God has dropped an angel among us. Andy was definitely an angel in my life.

Because I have sincerely realized Andy's time and purpose in my life, I have now realized something very important. We have all heard the cliché "It's never too late to change your life." This is true. I have also learned that it's never too late to change someone *else's* life.

I have been forever changed by Andy Anderson, and I have carried him with me for many years. He has stirred inside me feelings that have both shaped and moved me, feelings that *made* a difference in my life and thankfully, still do *make* a difference in my life. No matter who you are, you matter. And you make a difference. Every single one of us have the God-given potential to make a change in this world.

Just one more time, I wish I were driving from Vaught Hall down to New Dorm on the Ole Miss campus today. I wish I were pulling up in that red truck, stopping and letting Andy hop in to head home. I wish I could spend a few more hours just being with him. I'd love to thank him for all he was and is in my life, but then again, in his true fashion, Andy wouldn't let me.

Chapter Nineteen

Not From Memory, But From the Heart

---Bryan and Langdon---

Sunday, May 10, 1981. This was Mother's day. Approximately one month to the day earlier, President Ronald Reagan had signed Proclamation 4834, which in part stated:

> *They (mothers) shape the character of our people through the love and nurture of their children. It is the strength they give their families that keeps our Nation strong. On this Mother's Day, we express our deep personal gratitude to our own mothers and thank all those women whose devotion to their families helps sustain a healthy and productive citizenry. Now, Therefore, I, Ronald Reagan, President of the United States of America, do hereby designate Sunday, May 10, 1981, as Mother's Day. I direct Government officials to display the flag of the United States on all Federal Government buildings, and I urge all citizens to display the flag at their homes and other suitable places on that day.*

Andy did not display a flag that Sunday in May of 1981. Though if he had his eyesight, I

am sure he would have. But that didn't stop
Andy from a display or a special presentation of
his own.

Andy barely still maintained the ability to
get up and sit on the couch. It usually took all of
his energy, but nonetheless, he did just that. He
then asked his friend, John Gilbert, to go ask his
mom to come into the room.

As John tells it, he left Andy alone to go
and find Jo. They both came back into the room
where they sat down. Andy's mom let him know
he had her attention.

John recalls, "Jo Dorris and I were
greatly moved with tears of joy in our eyes and
we felt God's spirit in our midst, as we watched
Andy recite from his heart 1 Corinthians,
Chapter 13.

Love (New International Version)
1 If I speak in the tongues of men and of angels,
but have not love, I am only a resounding gong or
a clanging cymbal. 2 If I have the gift of prophecy
and can fathom all mysteries and all knowledge,
and if I have a faith that can move mountains,
but have not love, I am nothing. 3 If I give all I
possess to the poor and surrender my body to the
flames,[b] but have not love, I gain nothing.

4 Love is patient, love is kind. It does not envy,
it does not boast, it is not proud. 5 It is not rude,
it is not self-seeking, it is not easily angered, it
keeps no record of wrongs. 6 Love does not
delight in evil but rejoices with the truth. 7 It
always protects, always trusts, always hopes,
always perseveres.

8 Love never fails. But where there are prophecies, they will cease; where there are tongues, they will be stilled; where there is knowledge, it will pass away.
9 For we know in part and we prophesy in part,
10 but when perfection comes, the imperfect disappears. 11 When I was a child, I talked like a child, I thought like a child, I reasoned like a child. When I became a man, I put childish ways behind me. 12 Now we see but a poor reflection as in a mirror; then we shall see face to face. Now I know in part; then I shall know fully, even as I am fully known.

13 And now these three remain: faith, hope and love. But the greatest of these is love.

If it is true that the *gift* is in the *giver*,
then Andy makes it true that the giver *is* the gift.

Chapter Twenty

The First Chapter

---Bryan---

This story is not over. This may be the last chapter in this book but it may very likely be the first chapter to a newfound way of living and thinking for you. It certainly was for me. Andy's story is not over---it will never be over. Just as it has taken me thirty years to realize the awesome impact that Andy has been in my years past and now my years to come, I fully realize how his life has affected me in so many areas. Andy awakened something in me as a young man that I did not possess the day before he walked into that weight room.

His life was an example of a never-ending devotion to me, and his unselfishness always set the bar higher for someone like me. Because Andy wouldn't let me quit, I went on to play football at the University of Mississippi where I would become a three year starter for the Rebels. Not once in my years there did I think of quitting.

From there, I went on to begin many ordinary but extremely difficult jobs trying to break my way into the music business, where I would eventually find success and a career in songwriting. I would be blessed with being a writer on three number one records, have had

songs on over 30 million records sold, and would
be privileged to serve as part of the opening act
for Garth Brooks' World Tour for two years.
Since those days, I have authored two musical
plays, penned my first novel, and in between
tried my hand at everything from ice hockey to
rodeo. I have had many ups and twice as many
downs. But every time something seemed to be
impossible, I would think of my friend, my
buddy, my weight room and traveling partner,
Andy Anderson. I think of his attitude, his
example, and his never changing smile. I still
wear a cowboy hat to this day as it is a constant
reminder to me of my dear friend. I am a
different man because of Andy.

This story is not over. Andy has been
passed down to all I have met and ever will meet.
All I have shaken hands with, and all that have
seen me when I had the opportunity to quit, and
maybe even thought about it, or even tried, but
couldn't because Andy wouldn't let me.

I pray that this story keeps Andy's spirit
alive. You will face things that seem impossible,
things that hurt way down deep. And there will
be, no doubt, times when you will want to quit,
and it will make perfect sense that you do. I hope
you might close your eyes and see my friend walk
into the room. And then you may open your eyes
and see your own Andy walk into your life. My
Andy wore a cowboy hat, bandanna, and a letter
jacket. Yours will be dressed differently and you
may find him in your parents, grandparents,
friends, kids, teachers, coaches, neighbors---they
are everywhere.

When you are thinking you are doing all you can do and you are about to give up, I hope you see that smile and hear him ask you why you aren't doing more! I hope you might imagine him sitting himself in front of you, in front of your hurt, your injury, your pain. I hope you can see him push his pain aside to help you with yours. I hope he moves you to a different place, to a place you couldn't see yourself go. A better place. And I pray that if you ever think of quitting, God will put an angel in your life that won't let you, just like Andy wouldn't let me.

Andy Anderson Award

Robert William Anderson, Jr.
Class of 1979
June 3, 1961   October 18, 1981

It's usually when older people die that men talk about their contributions and the useful lives they lived.

Seldom does a young person pass away who leaves behind him many changed lives because of the way he gave himself to others.

Andy Anderson was this kind of young man. His life of 20 years was one of profound usefulness.

Beginning with those nearest him at home and reaching out to his fellow church members, his schoolmates and friends, and finally even to those in the community who did not know him personally, Andy's life touched and changed others.

Andy pointed others to God. It was his desire to see his friends grow in Christ. Andy continued to grow in his faith even in blindness in the last months of his life.

Those who know him best say it was his love—for God and others—that they will remember.

The community of Brentwood is a better place because Andy Anderson lived here.
Taken From Brentwood Journal

Works Cited

Steve & Annie Chapman, "I Am What You Are," *Steve & Annie Chapman*, 1981, Dawn Treader Music/BMI.

MistleToe Roaster. By Bryan Kennedy. John Lewis Auditorium. Staunton, VA. December 21, 2006.

Reagan, Ronald. <u>Proclamation 4834</u>. May 10, 1981.

The Holy Bible, New International Version. Thomas Nelson, 1984.

ABOUT THE AUTHORS

BRYAN KENNEDY was born in Shreveport, Louisiana but grew up in Tennessee in the Nashville area and is deeply rooted in the Country Music scene. His father is legendary record producer and Musician Hall of Fame member, Jerry Kennedy, and Bryan's songwriting successes span numerous country music artists. Bryan was the opening act for Garth Brooks' World Tour for two years singing and entertaining and is forever grateful to Garth for the wonderful ride. He's also had nine songs recorded by Garth Brooks including three #1 hits: "Good Ride Cowboy", "The Beaches of Cheyenne", and "American Honky Tonk Bar Association."

In addition to songwriting, Bryan has since completed two highly acclaimed musical comedy plays, *Toe Roaster* and *MistleToe Roaster*. Enjoying the success of these plays, he has also written two animated/cartoon scripts, two children books, and a mystery/suspense novel. Bryan continues to perform in his very own unique style of entertainment. To learn more about Bryan, please visit: *www.Bryan-Kennedy.com.*

LANGDON REID has used his multiple writing talents to find success in various fields. He is one-half of the country music duo Grandstaff, as he comes from Country Music heritage; his father is Don Reid, member of the Hall of Fame quartet, The Statler Brothers. Langdon has been performing and writing music since he was fourteen years old. He has had over 30 of his songs recorded by an assortment of artists in the country, bluegrass, and gospel fields, and has had freelance columns published in numerous newspapers and magazines. Langdon is the co-author of a Christmas book, *You Know It's Christmas When...*with his father Don and brother Debo. He is also an accomplished guitarist and vocalist.

Langdon serves as an elder and Sunday school teacher in his home church, Olivet Presbyterian. He lives with his wife, Alexis, and two children, Caroline and Davis, in Staunton, Virginia in the heart of the Shenandoah Valley. To learn more about him, please visit: www.WinkAtLife.com.